Suicide Salad

AMANDA WHITE

Suicide Salad

Contact the Author: SuicideSalad2021@gmail.com

ISBN: 978-0-620-96977-2 (e-book)

ISBN: 978-0-620-96976-5 (print)

Cover design by: Amanda White and Rod Torr

Published by **Perspective Publications**
Like us on Facebook @PerspectivePublications
https://www.facebook.com/PerspectivePublications
Website: https://perspective-pub.wixsite.com/perspective
Email: perspective.editorial@gmail.com

Suicide Salad – Amanda White

CONTENTS

ACKNOWLEDGEMENTS

Gratitude goes God's way first and it is with a grateful and humble heart that I am able to thank and express the sincerest dedications to the following angels who raise me up, inspire me and keep reminding me to keep on loving it all back to life.

Rod: for all the time in the world.

Jessica, Melissa, Mikayla, Angelique, Blair and Paige: my reasons for breathing.

Mark Wight: for adding years to a life on borrowed time.

Duncan Leyland and Martin Lewis for being angels for my angels.

All My Mom's & Dad's, Debbie Gunning, Leslie White, Lucille White, Michelle Middleton, Candida de Lange, Jade Bougaardt, David White, Alexa White, and Ami Gunning.

Sister Vee who walked through hell with and for me. Doreen Harty for always being atrue 'other mother'. Michael Trautman for pretty flowers on random days and unconditional love, and Roual Appel for guarding her last breath.

Sigi Klein, David Carew, William van Vuuren, John Hishin, Terry Ferreira, Melanie Carstens, Ronell Bowditch, Allyson Vine, Brother Judah & Sister Kim, Mike Shackleford, Lerato Rose, Colleen Williams, Florence Williams, Dom Lombard, Justine Meredith, Lauren Bremner, Kaylee Bremner, Kyra Shay Kennett, Sharon Tyler, Heidi Rutzen, Carolyn Axmann, Joe Lotter, Darren Posselthwaite, Heidi Rutzen, Lorraine Brooke-Sumner, Michelle Thompson, Janine Davidson, and Lizelle Coombs of Angels Resource Centres, and all those who know their names belong here.

MESSAGE FROM THE AUTHOR

"Human resilience seems miraculous to me.
I listen to people's stories and am moved in awe at what
they have suffered.
After heart-breaking loss, they rise once again
and greet the day,doing what needs to be done to care for
themselves, others and the world.

How can we fail to be in awe of how tenaciously life
urges us to touch, taste, listen and breathe in the day,
even after pain has brought us to our knees?
And on any given day, when some cannot rise, we lean
into each other—taking turns at rising, sharing the
resilience
that is part of our nature."
~*Oriah Mountain Dreamer*~

When the soul speaks, is it a whisper or is it a scream?
Is there applause at the eventual and long awaited
awakening, or just a silent, grateful acceptance of the
learnings and the rememberings foretold as we inhale our

first new breath and exhale all else that our former selves were disillusioned by.

I have walked through the valleys of the shadows of death on many occasions, and I know and always have that the will of God will never lead me where the grace of God hasn't kept and continues to keep me.

This is my attempt to tame the world as I share a journey. Or was that a few? My greatest desire is for all of us to embrace the wild within ourselves; to perhaps tame the wild in me and wild the tame in you.

Life's challenges do not always manifest as natural disasters or acts of God. Each one of us will have to face a multitude of disasters in our lifetimes, mostly when least expected. Even when expected, these remain no less challenging. Sometimes it's the loss of a loved one, job, or even the loss of faith. It could be having to abandon one's home due to unfair persecution at the hands of an unscrupulous landlord, acting in cahoots with a corrupt judge. Or ending up homeless. Some disasters may seem smaller at first glance, but can feel just as significant such as a failed class, a disastrous stage play, or getting passed over for a first prize when you know you deserve the trophy or 'player of the match' award.

All of us face disasters sooner or later, in some form or another. A life completely void of disasters is a fantasy, as are the movies too many of us wish we lived in where everything works, nothing explodes, hearts never get broken, and we all live happily ever after.

In the business world, teams of risk management specialists conduct in-depth surveys to prepare emergency survival kits, and draw up plans and strategies covering everything from health and safety to industrial and/or political relations.

Unfortunately for too many of us trying to manage our own balancing acts, we are ultimately left to our own devices when these devastations happen, and we need to be reminded that we may and can reach out, hold hands, and help ourselves and each other up.

However, in order to take that first step, we need to surrender to the fact that we need to face forward and humbly reach for and grab those invisible, outstretched hands. Pull, push, and pull some more. Push a little longer and then continue to dig, delve, and reach for the maps we are offered along the way—or at least until we find our own inner compass to guide us in reaching whatever our 'next' is.

A sister reminds, *"if you're going through hell, just keep going."* There are perhaps too many choices available in our age. With no GPS or tracking device provided on installation of the programs that we are governed/run by, we have to use our own inner guidance systems. This is required, especially when the road we're on leads us to the odd fork we may have to veer towards, without the chainsaws needed to first get through the forest of thorns, bushes, and fallen trees up ahead.

The other fork is the one you're almost certain you just

managed to get yourself off of.

Can we ever really be prepared for disaster? Or do we just need to remember or be reminded that we were in fact always prepared, and that our blades just needed sharpening before the inevitable clearing of the 'deadery' and the ultimate becoming (or was that unbecoming?) of ourselves?

As I lay these pages before you, I believe that you will find that piece of yourself, the broken part, the one that went missing when all of this shit started. Enlightened, you will let it return itself to you who, in turn, will accept all the love you have to give back to your inner child, as well as your ancient self.

As I arrive from the darkness and embrace the light that I am, I look forward to saluting each and every one of you on the paths along our journey that will no doubt cross along the way.

This is not a religious book, but reaches into the depths of my own spirit and the spirituality that has always been part of me, and which inner light and spirit is the reason I am able to have reached this place to say : YOU CAN, YOU WILL, YOU MUST.

Perhaps it's not possible for you to believe, but it is time. Maybe the end of this fork in the road has arrived and you're simply too weary to notice or lift another limb, except for one last attempt at movement which is to kick the chair that you're standing on, out from under you as your need for death remains greater than your need for life.

I will then ask a favor, and that would be for you to stay with me long enough for me to read you this book and be comforted that I'm holding you with each and every word, as we walk each other home where our soul tribes await their celebration of you. You are never alone.

I will no doubt offend and rip off some old scabs, perhaps even give you some new ones. I offer no apology. Be as brave as you were always meant to be and look to the Source that is You, if that's what you have come to find out.

This book has been organized as a series of accounts taken from various chapters of my life. Spanning across a small lifetime from a 'hatchling' to my current, mostly blessed and mostly healed self, I use my life and the encounters that it contained to show the power of human resilience, love and faith, and for you to see and know that everything is possible and everything can be overcome: together.

These accounts are not in order of events and here is no beginning, middle, or end. It is still going on. Always starting, stopping, re-starting, going on and on and on in the circle of life that is ours to be blessed, chosen, privileged, and worthy of our participation.

Will you come on this journey with me?

A WORD OF CAUTION

This may or may not be the most inappropriate thing you'll ever read as its contents are strewn out across the blank pages before me, and I'm compelled to say it like it is. I don't know how else to do this.

I'm sure I would hazard a good guess what your reactions will be as I, like you, have lived through many loads of dirty washing. If we do not treat it with the right soap, fabric softener, bleach or stain remover, it will be rendered unusable and will be hung out to be aired for no other reason than to assist you in deciding your next course of action.

We are left with a few choices: We can either toss it out (waste), use it for rags to clean something/ anything/ everything (recycle/clean), or sew the pieces back together to make a patchwork blanket (create) for that lonely vagrant under the bridge, who may be colder than you this season, and who craves simply to know what that thing called 'compassion' may taste like on the way in and not only on the way out.

1:   NOTE TO SELF

So what started with a letter to my Ancient Self (whichever self that was with whom I was supposed to speak) turns out will be a longer note than anticipated. Three hours is not nearly enough to capture the moments of the life you're about to lead, or even help you make that deadline for the essay you have to read aloud to the class: the one you never handed in for fear of what the teacher might think or the students might make a mockery of or laugh at.

Tasked with the exercise of writing a letter to my younger self by taking a photograph from younger days, I respond as follows:

Hey, I remember 18-year-old You!

I thought you'd want to know a few things ahead of time. Not to persuade you to do things differently, as I know you probably wouldn't. Perhaps just to help to remind you to pack lightly as you learn to eventually be free enough to leave the unwanted baggage behind.

Someone will tell you one day that you're a 'Volunteer Soul' and that you're here again by choice. I still have no idea why any person would voluntarily do 'this' again. The photograph shows you at 18 with a nervous smile. You almost bite through your lip. Your eyes are bright and alive, and you're completely excited for the unknown that you've decided to venture towards. You are fascinated, petrified, and everything in-between.

Saying goodbyes again. Mom says, "Goodbye, my little bird. Return to the nest any time you want." Feeling brave, on a day when you change your name to Mandi with an 'I' instead of Mandy with a 'why?' you take flight.

A myriad of emotions engulf you all at once. Your heart races as a car horn blows in the driveway. You pick up your handbag and head for the open door, feeling like a puppy who just realized that someone left the gate open.

In later years, she will whisper sarcastically, "Goodbye, have a nice life."

You can't wait to leave.

You'll have a phenomenally fun career. Despite not having finished school and working since you were a mere fifteen years old, you know all about having to pay your dues. You will make a great success in whatever you choose to do. You'll have to have lots of jobs. Not because you've ever been dismissed (albeit a couple of 'amicable settlements') but because your Gemini spirit needs and thrives on constant change and you get used to life giving you a regular jolt. A cubicle staring at a purple wall and a computer screen all day will kill your spirit. Don't wait too long to get yourself out of claustrophobic spaces.

You love everybody. There may be a few 'haters' who cannot help but adore your mischievous, tenacious, and adventurous spirit. It will get you into the principal's office more than he chooses to see you. Nonetheless, he enjoys the entertainment and gladly welcomes your return. Don't beat yourself up about it for too long though because you'll just realize it was a waste of time anyway, and perhaps you will reach the place you will find yourself in a lot sooner if you hadn't unnecessarily beat yourself up so badly. You will sometimes find yourself in shallow waters but will always find the way to wade yourself out superficially unscathed.

You will assist in the creation of three exquisitely beautiful daughters, who all lead you to a state of perfect grace as you bear their sorrows, hopes, and dreams. They will be your legacy and your 'Noloyiso's Voice'. Who is Noloyiso? you will ask. Alas, here I will tease and you'll need to wait. You'll meet her for the most perfect moments when the time is right. She will walk back and find you wherever you are and with broken, bleeding feet and a wounded soul, she will ultimately be your healing as she has and always will be. Always remember that, every single day of your life. The butterflies await your becoming.

You have beautiful granddaughters and, if it's meant to be, there may be a few grandsons. You become 'mother' to many as you stand firm in your belief that it takes a village to raise a child, and will be ever grateful to the 'other mothers' in your own daughters' lives. You will always choose to live in a world of no judgment, and believe that you should always remember to not judge, lest ye be judged, as you will and have been.

But head's up!! Your life will take you down a road much like your mother's, perhaps like none other. You will lose lovers, family, friends, and the presence of too many who will always be dear to you. Just keep reminding yourself that *"we never silently stop loving those we once loved out loud"*, as I read somewhere once.

You will learn to switch off as you endure ten years of beatings of the maddest and hardest kind. Stay strong. Prepare. You will suffer inquisitions. Tell your children their father hanged himself. Tell them their grandfather hanged himself, too. Be hated by your children; be loved by your children.

You will flee promises and go on many road trips until you find yourself holding your mother's icy cold hand at her murder scene. With a brown leather belt still wrapped around her throat, covered in a blue blanket, you will look down and know that she has finally left that place that had been her torment for thirty years. She is gang raped by three men, and beaten to death by the very same homeless people she took in off a cold street, giving refuge on a dark night. A terrible tragedy. An ironic peace. A story worthy of its own chapters.

To add insult to the injuries, your brother will kill your

mother's life partner six weeks later when it is alleged that he paid to have her killed, and will be sent to prison for another thirty-one years. You get through this. Your brother does too, somehow. Your mother's killers are still free thanks to the maladies of justice. A family torn apart, a family joined together. A family eternally changed.

Eighteen months later, you will search for sixteen long days to find your daughter. The longest days of your life pass while she is kidnapped, beaten, stabbed, and raped repeatedly, by more than forty demons who keep her drugged and tortured for longer than any horror movie should last. She is found wandering on a street by an angel whose name you forget, on a day when you scream with every breath in your being for her to just call you. She survives this, and lives long enough to allow herself to be loved back to life, until she finally finds the strength to go to the place where she can once again be held in her father's arms. The father of her first betrayal. Her first love. As love returns itself to itself.

Six months pass until the day arrives where your soul is left feeling wasted and barren as you open the door and are faced with the sight of your beautiful child hanging dead from a beam as she finally frees herself from her nightmares.

Your prayer will be answered with the last exhale of her breath as your deafening screams are heard, and echo in the halls of time forever. You will scatter your mother's and daughter's ashes from the same mountain and across the same seas, and you will eventually learn to breathe as you write their names in the sand, on the beach below a perfect window by the light of every full moon. You survive everything, even this, for which no previous traumas could have prepared you for even if it was, perhaps morbidly, expected.

You will find yourself holding a gun in your own mouth as you feel the world has completely annihilated you, and the scars on your wrist remind you of having overcome everything. Your children are always a beautiful reminder that you just have to wake up every day. Just for a while longer; as you know that you'll have to teach them young that we are only borrowed to each other for moments and that everyone goes away. Treasure every last one.

Life excites you, life abandons you, and life entices you. Your wild spirit frees you and opens your world and mind to places where you know you've seen God, and too often leaves you saying, "I'm only watching this movie." That phrase keeps you going. Learn it young.

You never really have to put the TV on. You've got your own reality show. As life disappoints and leaves you breathless and wasted in its wake, you'll see a new sunrise every morning and you will know that, eventually, you do get to realize the dreams and miracles life will bring you.

And then, remind me on another day to tell you about the pit stops and the road trips. Be sure to pass them on to your grandchildren and theirs. Those too may blow your mind.

Waterproof mascara, whiskey and eye drops are good allies to help mask what's behind a smile that, on some days, is so unbearably hard to wear. Yours is a world full of family, friends, lovers, and crazy characters that are right there with you all along, even when you can't see or feel them. You will meet the sisters and the angels that will carry you. Don't ostracize anyone and always stay in touch. I tell you this now, for fear you learn this too late. Footprints in the sand become your daily miracle. You make a few bad choices and plenty of mistakes, but your kindness, love and sense of humor help you as you wander your way through the world, enlightened and inspired by everything. Always wanting the world and all who share the space to be treated with compassion, empathy, and kindness. Always remain humble: every time an old lady tells you that same old story as the week before, as you watch her memories fade and smile as you know she may never remember you, and know that those were the fingerprints you will always talk about and want to leave. Don't smoke in bed. Sometimes even the bravest firemen will sleep through a burning bed. And remember to back up your documents!

You will need a spinal fusion by the time you're forty-five as well as have osteoarthritis, a hiatus hernia, nerve damage to your coccyx area, and would have had countless operations. Be mindful of your health, learn self-defense, and go to the doctor sooner rather than later. Your physical challenges will not, however, bring you down and you get through it, whatever 'it' may be.

Respect every moment for what it holds, and remember to breathe.

Look after your feet, they will need to carry you far, dear sweet child who too often feels that everyone seems to forget but will eventually remember her. Know that you grow from that dear sweet child to an all knowing, enlightened woman.

You meet some of the lovers of your dreams (and too many of your nightmares), but the Grace of God appears in the form of a beautiful, mysterious, protective, loving, kind being at a time when you are your most beautiful mess. This mystical union again entices and leads you to look up, holds your hand, and reminds you to breathe. It gives you different reasons to keep getting there, even when you are being your most awful self. He reminds you that your other daughters need you too and that you shouldn't leave anyone behind. This relationship will also come with its comedic challenges, but you know that this is the one who alone occupies that space in your soul reserved for him until the exhale of your very last breath and your most final touch. He is Love as are you, and should fate decide otherwise and another moment granted, you can trust that he will remain by your side as he has. If it's only for a brief moment in time, this memory you will hold closest. Don't be too hard on him. He's worth it. At least that's what the heart speaks. Don't be surprised if tomorrow you feel the complete opposite, it's just another you tripping you up. Be Nice. Trust the beauty of broken English and the language of the heart, even when he's being his most frustratingly Cancerian self. This will be a clumsy, crazy union. Soul mate? Perhaps, you will wonder, as it tumbles and jumbles and tests your patience, and completes your world.

There will be stories more horrific, beautiful, and inspiring than yours, but it's your salt that proves your worth and you're worth every pinch. Just know that. It all gets answered. You never seek sympathy. It's both never and always exactly what the Gemini in you will need. Don't hang around for that either, you'd feel just as misunderstood. You don't do self-loathing, even when you find yourself in your darkest spaces—it's just who you are. You may offend some, but only until you've been your most offended, and there you will find pieces of yourself, too.

Fasten your seatbelt. It's guaranteed to be a bumpy ride with, hopefully, no more police tape or blue blankets. Expect some turbulence. Be Strong. Be Guided. Let me hold your hand.

With all my Love,
Me

A longer PS:

It will be worth it. Just don't stop getting there, even when life brings you to your knees, breaks your heart, and shows you there is life after death, after all. Always expect that place where love returns itself to itself to reveal itself to you, as it always will. It is a magical place.

And, as you knowingly emerge, intrinsically changed at the core, you will attract all that you came back here to get. Hmm, what could that possibly be?

What happens next? I guess we'll have to watch this space.

Be Brave, Always.

You will be wondering, "How old am I when I teach myself these things?" and I may answer, "Oh, maybe a thousand and something", maybe only forty-five years old. Maybe just a five-year-old standing outside her parents' bedroom door as her mother's screams are heard splitting the silence in the dead of another scary night.

You will find yourself sitting helpless and abandoned as you are dragged by the hair down a lonely street one moonless night, just to prove someone's point.

Always know that when the Ancients call your name, you will be ready and, eventually, you will know that you were once terrified, but no longer find yourself in that place.

You know how to love. You wish a million wishes to still come true. You are afraid of not much else. You feel strongly that a story has to be told and that you are now able to tell it.

And, in the moment of my unbecoming, I will perhaps teach you what I should have taught you long before.

Namaste

Now step onto that plane and make the most of the flight. You are loved. Whatever you do, just don't join the nunnery!!!

February 2016…

2:   WHEN ANGELS TAKE FLIGHT

"Loss pushes us to difficult places where we have not been before. We often question whether or not we have the courage and stamina to survive the pain. However, we often are given gifts that tell us that we are not alone and that we can withstand the journey." ~*Susan Barbara Apollon*~

I remember being about eight years old when I attended my first funeral of one of the elders. I no longer recall who but Aunt Grace comes to mind or was that Uncle George?

A cousin and I were reprimanded for giggling at the back of the church, either at some other aunt's awful attempt at song or another's beehive hairdo. We were too young to really understand what was really going on. We just knew that we didn't really mean to laugh. It just sounded or looked so funny and we could not stop the giggles. Needless to say, parents and elders weren't impressed. I always thought that if Aunt Grace (or Uncle George) had heard or seen it, they would have probably done the same. I know now that, despite the inappropriate timing, those giggles distracted a few over-broken hearts for a few moments and gave them time to breathe, as I too would encounter moments when my over-broken heart needed to be distracted by a smile or a giggle.

A cousin is electrocuted to death by the electrical cabling at a train station when being chased by muggers at the age of nineteen.

A favorite uncle was taken from us by cancer, leaving a mother of five to raise her bunch alone.

When I was twenty-one years old, my beautiful step-mother passed away from cancer at the young age of thirty-four. I was faced with heartache and I internalized this and showed only strength to my husband and children, leaving it up to time to heal this wound. My father's heart breaking was too much to witness or bear as Pavarotti consoled us with *Nessun Dorma*. Perhaps my father also died that day, I consider in hindsight as I watch him spend the remainder of his life pretty much in the role as widow, albeit with a few romantic interludes.

The same year, a dear friend miscarried twins a month before they were due to be born.

A beloved friend was killed in a car accident one night during a drunken drive home, the only car on a dark and lonely road.

At one stage, I wondered whether I was a bad omen to have so many people passing away around me, so I spent many years isolating myself and shied away from visiting too many people. It was only later I learned and believed that none of these had anything to do with me and that it was just part of life as we paid our respects to a beautiful grandmother, a grandfather and other elders who shared our lives and were our role models and mentors.

Thirty years on and I am not surprised when overhearing someone's comment that 'death follows that lady', or let myself be offended by any comment from those less informed. No shit! You think I wasn't freaked out enough at the thought that I was maybe a jinx? I went on to spend more than enough years keeping away from the world as much as possible, just in case. Mom nicknaming me the 'black widow' in hindsight seems fitting.

'Good Samaritan Brutally Murdered' read the headlines printed beneath a picture of my own mother on the front page of a local newspaper.

A niece's outrage fills the lines of another newspaper as she recounts how my mother was raped and murdered on 5th November 2012. She was a 62-year-old grandmother who was strangled to death and sexually assaulted on her farm by a homeless couple she 'rescued' from the streets and offered accommodation in a cabin on her property. Four men and one woman were involved in this brutal tragedy. Prior to her murder, she had taken in a young woman and her two children who she'd found begging at traffic lights nearby. The couple told her that they had lost all their belongings in a fire. The woman was pregnant. My aunt helped the woman while she was in labor and the baby was delivered by my niece in the same room that would be her final resting place.

As a family, we cared for the little family she had adopted. The woman lured her out of the house by knocking on her bedroom window and asking her to open because she needed to get supplies for the baby. My mother's partner was woken up by the couple and two men who told him that "she was lying dead in the shed". She was found with a pillowcase over her head and a belt around her neck. Four suspects were arrested and detained for a crime described as "shocking, scary and cruel".

Nine months later they were released when the DNA evidence went missing and the investigating officer Inspector failed to attend the court proceedings, resulting in the criminals being released until the State was in a position to prove their case. These criminals have been released back into society because someone failed to ensure her rights. The recent ruling adds a stain to an already painful memory as we are still reminded that she has ultimately still been dishonored as her killers play for time and after eight or so years it is seemingly doing nothing more than becoming another cold case, receiving the least attention and zero by a once interested press looking for sensational headlines to lure readers. Nearly a decade later and the case is still awaiting attention, and time leaves it as cold as it left her.

The killers in the process continue to avoid being sent to a maximum security facility, possibly the same one that housed my brother. Where karma perhaps waits out her time until she returns with her appropriate serving—or was that her appropriate serving returning to be served up to her?

I had already buried so many loved ones and found myself more than drinking my way to and through the nexts which would include my mother's memorial service. My 'stepfather' a few weeks later, and the subsequent loss of my brother to a lifetime of incarceration for his choice to become Karma, and ensure that retribution not be denied for this, as he shoots our 'stepfather' in the head and is sentenced to thirty one years in a maximum security prison.

It was not to end there: my youngest daughter was abducted eighteen months later after going missing for a lifetime of days and nights spent staring at a clock and seeing a billion seconds creep slowly around a clock, whose time appeared to have stopped at first glance. She is found, brought home, and decides to take flight from life six months later when her reflection in the mirror becomes too much for her to look at. Another case gets left to freeze over because she never could make that statement to the detectives, nor would I allow her to.

The following year, another beautiful aunt succumbed to cancer the day after my birthday, fortunately only a few months of suffering before her inevitable demise.

A friend dies of a heart attack on the platform of a train station and we wait patiently with his body until the paramedics arrive. I thank God for the knowledge that 'unnatural causes' will not be the words reflected on these death certificates.

I made the decision to deal with my life in a more sober frame of mind as I slowed down on the drinking, starting to succumb to the sense of actually feeling those things I'd avoided in favor of the blur. No amount of medicated practice runs working through the grieving process could prepare me for the raw, savage assault of doing it without daily drinking or a fix of some sort as I chose to try to be more present and clear-headed, more often than not.

It took a whole lot longer, and it did start feeling a lot more challenging burying a child compared to a husband, mother, father, friends, or lovers. It seemed too hard as I stepped out of one life filled with children's laughter into another where I couldn't face being in the company of any children and avoided them as much as possible.

I desperately wanted to reach out to my children and do whatever it took to absorb their pain as I had done when their father took flight, but I could not. I found myself withdrawing and avoiding them for way too long because I thought that I would only add to their hurt. I was comforted that they each had significant others to hold them in the silent spaces I had left in my absence from their worlds. I knew that their own children would fill their lives, time, and hearts with abundant eternal love, as they in turn allowed me to navigate my way back to them through the sea of tears we shared.

In the haze of the hundreds of days that have gone by,

I somehow managed to clear the mist and started to see again. The words that evaded my mind for so very long appeared and the words on the pages I was always meant to fill, slowly started forming until I reached that place where I could once again pick up my pen and start telling the stories I am meant to tell.

I needed to reach a place where I had free hands, open arms, and a replenished heart. I attempted to make my way back. I had to have faith that my girls would be okay during a longer than anticipated leave of absence, as I undertook the journeys I would find myself taking to get through to the other side of the homeless state of my heart.

In my quest to understand why I was still here, learning how to process the losses of loved ones, I came to understand that all life is to be respected and cherished, knowing that we are borrowed to each other for moments. Whether our moments last five minutes, five hours, five days, or fifty years, these are the moments we are granted. No matter how, when, why, or what, we all die at the time we are called.

An unexpected challenge arrives with the newness of the feelings that come with the recent loss of a best friend. It shocks and overwhelms me, despite all who had already gone before or how many practice runs I may have already had with the grieving process.

A cousin and his father-in-law are lost to the Coronavirus, and we silently mourn in unison, unable to attend his funeral in support of his family—a reality too many families have already had to face.

I know that soon there will be more fallen angels (and a few demons) who will get their wings as age, disease, and a world pandemic claim them, too. Perhaps I'll see you again before your form loses its shape. Perhaps not. Perhaps I'll have the time to say an earthy goodbye and you'll see me mouth the words. Perhaps not.

I do know another thing for sure, and that is I have seen, I have listened, I have loved, I've lived, and I've heard. I have died a thousand times. Perhaps I'll die a thousand more as I carry the memory of the faces and places that are etched in the lines of my mind and buried deep within my soul.

I always know that those little things that I alone see aren't by chance and that the signs, the dragonflies, the whisper, the song, the daisy, the Monarch, or those random pennies which my angels use to remind me of the promise that my streets will always be paved with gold. The wind whispers her assurance that they are always with me. My angels will do anything to reach me; to give me hope, keep me on track, and help when I allow life to let me forget.

How did I get through all these things? There were and would always be different how's and different why's. No choice nor event is less significant or meaningful than another.

Amongst the lines strewn across the pages you now hold in your hand, you will find those pearls of wisdom that may resonate with you, and which you can grab onto to try to help yourself out of the darker places life can sometimes take you to.

I wish you Bravery.

3:   SUICIDE NOTES

The semi-colon (;) is the internationally recognized symbol for suicide survivors. It is tattooed as a promise to the self to carry on the rest of the (Life) sentence, because there's still something to be said before the absolute end as would be indicated by the full stop. If for no other reason than to take that gulp of air as we try to squeeze the last bit of life into (or was that out of?), the sentence.

I could not ever say that I was either for or against suicide. I had seen justifiable reasons for such final steps, and obvious sense could be made of some. No sense could be made of others' seemingly selfish or cowardly behavior, as it is oftentimes seen, and we could only speculate as to their motivation.

There were those that I managed to convince to share more of their moments with the world. I still needed to make sense of the long line of suicides and fatalities that had touched my life, and gave me reason to dig deeper to try to understand, or to make sense of others' journeys to the darkest places a mind can go to, come out of or get stuck in.

I   encountered   more   than   enough   homeless   or

imprisoned hearts that also needed comfort, as we shared and bore each other's bloodied and tear-stained cores with whatever we had left to hold on with.

Various people from all walks of life, all ages, colors, or creeds crossed my path who had attempted, or at the very least considered, ending their own lives, or were survivors of suicide. I knew there had to be a reason for still being around and knew that I had always been put exactly where I was needed. Some I saved, and some I could not. Through it all, I knew that I only ever had one chance at possibly changing a stranger's desired end result back into love, encouragement, and comfort, as I welcomed him or her back to life; to try my best to give hope where there was no hope before and to offer a hand to the ones who no longer wanted to reach their natural finish line.

I was fourteen when my first boyfriend, one of a set of twins, hung himself with a coat hanger in his navy barracks. He was nineteen years old. No reason was given to me as Freddie Mercury belted out The Show Must Go On over the radio and my heart wailed in harmony with Bohemian Rhapsody.

At fifteen, I found myself at my own mother's bedside as she lay in a coma for three days after a massive overdose of prescription medication. Apparently not her first, but another failed attempt. Not sure if it was her last? Twenty-seven years later, I would find myself wishing it were her bedside and not her dead side.

At seventeen, I found myself saying goodbye to a dear

friend who, always the joker, will always be remembered by me as 'Our April Fool', as he lay on the railway tracks not far from our home and waited for the first train just past midnight. Only it wasn't an April Fool's joke—he was identified by the remains of his clothing only. Head, legs, and an arm severed from his core. He was twenty-three-years-old.

I recall him telling me broken bits of stories about how he had gotten involved with drugs, drinking, and a group of satanists. I recall him telling me how he had witnessed, and participated in, some grim rituals. He tried in vain to get out and away, but it was too late—he had gotten involved with dark forces who had overpowered him and claimed his soul and robbed him of his light. He was powerless and lost. Forever. It was the only way he knew how to get out. No amount of drinking or drugs could drown out the visuals that had appeared before him at his own, albeit ignorant and perilously curious, hand.

I remember being cautioned at about fifteen to always be cautious with my curiosity and to never delve into the darker things in the world. 'Never get into anything you don't have the power to get out of' always echoed in my mind, until I was sure that I had developed sufficient insight, power, and divine protection.

My first boss, and one of my earliest mentors, left work one afternoon after being a part of my life for about ten years, and shot himself in the head. He was sixty-eight and, already having passed retirement age, I suspect he was still too young to stop working at the prescribed 65 or was possibly ill—one could speculate about a few variables as we would not be privy to the contents of the single note left in his briefcase for his wife. A most unexpected act from a seemingly 'normal', functional, dynamic person with the greatest zest for life and an inspiration to many.

I thought I knew what it was like to battle with my own dark places—until I found myself being rushed to hospital in an ambulance, my first attempt consisting of a deeply slit wrist carved up while on a cocktail of gin, a whole array of tranquilizers, and an aunt's collection of heart/lung medication. As I had no parents or older siblings around, the choice was mine as to the treatment offered. Pump my stomach and an admission to the Psych Ward? None of the above was my response as they sewed up the deepest cut and I remember waking up, horribly ill, at home. My baby sister easily took on the big sister role and spent her stopover on her way to London, nursing me, caring for me as I filled bucket after bucket in a marathon vomiting session.

I was twenty-eight years old and tired of life, having run away from my husband and children to end my life. I failed at this too and had to endure the humiliation I felt, together with the lonely, broken state of my heart, as my husband asked what the hell I thought I was doing. He had to come to terms with the mayhem I had left behind by this most unexpected act, by actions he would never have understood because, on the outside, all was well and he was completely oblivious to anything being out of place.

Two years later, he hanged himself in his garage. Or did he? The discovery fourteen years later of an insurance policy that had been cashed out by a friend all those years before made one wonder. A vision I'd brushed aside was recalled from years before in which said friend was sitting on top of him, pinning his shoulders down with his knees, while the hands around his throat squeezed until there was no breath. This 'friend' allegedly found him, cut him down, and attempted CPR in vain. I would always wonder whether there was foul play when his remains were cremated too quickly to enable the autopsy I tried to insist upon to rule out any foul play. I would always be curious about said friend's involvement.

From this point, I found myself getting a first-hand education at what it was like to live with what was left behind, as I taught my children what I had learned: that everyone goes away.

Here too began what would become a fourteen year suicide watch over my own baby girl, who was only eight years old when her father took flight two days after her birthday. One of his last notes was written on her birthday (our wedding anniversary). I never could show it to her and she never knew of its existence. Another note was left for his mother, which ended with a 'fuck you for my life'. The absence of a letter for me I never questioned; he didn't need to say a thing.

A year later, his own father and my children's

grandfather climbed up a bell tower in Spain and hanged himself.

A 'people's hero' and dear friend slits his own throat on Valentine's Day, and hearts are again broken and lives shattered. What could possibly drive one who had everything one could ask for, millions in the bank, a thriving psychology practice and world fame to such a final act? A broken heart?

A friend and business partner ties himself to a shark net and drowns himself in my hometown the day after Christmas of the same year.

A mother-in-law, comforted that her only son would be held in the safe arms of the earth angels that gathered around closer than ever, overdosed and ended up in hospital. She died a week or so later due to some alleged hospital staff member's negligence while she was recovering.

By the age of thirteen, my youngest daughter had tried to hang herself on three occasions (that I knew of) and had cut herself many times up her one arm. I found myself promising her that if I found her like that again, I would let her bleed. I would not call for help and would hold her hand until she was gone, because I understood and respected that her need for death was, and always had been, greater than her need for life as she claimed responsibility for the death of her father. At twenty, she would ask if I would still keep my promise. At twenty-one years old, she frees me from having to keep and respect her honor by keeping a never-forgotten promise which she knew I'd keep, no matter how hard a request it may have been.

A niece pleads, "I can't do it anymore!" Many years of caring for her blind, autistic, non-verbal son, twenty-four hours a day, as well as a two-year-old, while having to navigate her way through a challenging and sometimes most volatile marriage, had taken its toll. She felt terrible admitting this to me after my daughter and her cousin's own suicide because she had always portrayed the strongest exterior to unknowing onlookers. Five years on and I am still glad that her heroic insistence to persevere has kept her in our lives and that of her children.

I was approached to chat to a young girl in the psychiatric ward of a local hospital who had tried to kill herself for the eighth time by the age of sixteen. The rope she tried to hang herself with broke. I had half an hour's visit in which I could possibly help this beautiful young soul that, at sixteen, she still had much to live for, even when it was the last thing she could believe. Her father had molested her as a girl: the first betrayal. She was conflicted as to her sexual identity, a reality to which her religious parents were vehemently opposed. A few years later, she takes up with a homeless drug addict and falls pregnant. At least the appearance of not being gay placates her family. I always wonder how she really is and what traumas she would have to deal with at a later stage of her life, as she again reaches out to me after being raped on a nearby beach on her way to get drugs for her partner. Her little boy, however, brings her joy and fills her otherwise muddied world with light and the inspiration to keep on keeping on.

I find myself counselling a young lady in a police cell. Saving souls and chasing dragons in a prison cell seems the next 'assignment'. Oh Lord, that looked eerie. I watched another visitor from hell take her place as she consumed the smuggled heroin and transformed her own lifeless form into a darkened monster that seemed to slither through and out of her. The night before, she had tried unsuccessfully to slit her wrists with a plastic spoon. I watch over her for forty-eight hours and leave her with a prayer and the hope that I will see her again when she is released. A week later, a knock on the door brings relief when her daughter comes to thank me for not letting her mom die.

The rope around the neck of another young man is cut just in time as a father finds him. He could no longer bear being without his young son as the mother removes herself from his life and threatens that he wouldn't see his son again.

The desperate screams of another son as he discovers his mother has overdosed wakes me from the room next to mine at the boarding house we shared. The effects of too many years of drug and other addictions and other familial traumas finally tipping the scales of how much more heartache she believed she could possibly bear. Her attempt was unsuccessful and her life granted more breath.

She overcomes and grows and inspires daily.

A real challenge comes six years after burying my youngest child, when another daughter makes an unsuccessful attempt at slitting her wrists after too many conversations insisting that she'd rather kill herself and her children than to cope with her life. The thought of losing another daughter is almost too much to comprehend. She was mostly apologetic for putting me through such trauma and, once again, filling my head with the sight and silences brought on by the memory of her sister hanging dead from a beam.

Her challenge: to keep living, as do I and many others, even when she's running out of breath. She is my hero on more days than she could ever begin to fathom.

A heroin addict once told me, "one wrong word and you kill people". I responded by asking whether they weren't, in fact, already dead or dying, anyway. He was the only one left out of their original group of twenty-two friends who spent their lives in and out of hell. He was dying too and all he wanted was his life back. It was too late.

M Scott Peck suggests in '*Further Along The Road Less Travelled*' that "you strike up a serious relationship with the end of your existence. Like any great love, death is full of mystery and that's where much of the excitement comes from. Because as you struggle with the mystery of your death, you will discover the meaning of your life."

He teaches further that "we cannot live with courage

and confidence until we can have a relationship with our own death indeed, we cannot live fully unless there is something that we are willing to die for."

I have been in the darkest places a mind can go to, I have lived through many attempted and successful suicides, so have every idea of what you are feeling as I too have made a few failed attempts.

A few things to consider when it comes to the various methods adopted:

More people start an attempt and abort it rather than carry it through. There are methods that can be interrupted without harm mid-attempt, such as overdose, cutting, CO poisoning, and hanging/suffocation, which all offer a window of opportunity for rescue or change of heart that guns or jumps do not.

Do note that a method that requires technical knowledge is less accessible than one that does not. Given the brief duration of some suicidal crises, a lethal dose of pills in the nightstand poses a greater danger than a prescription that must be hoarded over months to accumulate a lethal dose. Similarly, a gun in the closet poses a greater risk than a very high bridge five miles away, even if both methods have equal lethality if used.

Method One: Hanging

To ensure success, the correct equipment is required in accordance with timing preferences, i.e. quick, hangout for a few moments, or slow, etc.

Note that nylon rope is easily obtained anywhere and remember our eco-friendly advice to always recycle our waste.

Practice! Practice! Practice! No man, not the deed. Just tying knots. That noose must work. A grumpy noose could mean you might still get a few more minutes out of your unread or unwritten sentence; to consider you've always got a chance to change, but procrastination is a bitch and the desired result will be achieved if it is your fate; if it is your time; if… if… if…

Remember that the cord or rope you choose to use is the one that will cut your life supply and must be strong enough as to not break. If you have to first lose weight and shed some stuff, give it more time—or get a stronger rope.

Make sure that the beam/branch/bar/balcony used to tie the rope to is going to (a) going to hold your body weight; and (b) that whatever you stand or stack to stand on to get high enough to get the job done, is solid. Definitely a red-faced moment if you fuck yourself up first and are found on floor with neck still entangled, sprawled on floor, concussed and NOT DEAD YET. You got your worst undies on 'cos you thought "if I'm dead it won't matter". You wake up after a three day concussed nap with a broken nose, bruised voice, broken toe, no coma, and no memorial with yellow tulips. Not even a slight bit of amnesia.

The possibility exists that your soul wouldn't let your

spirit let go but, during an argument, it held on just to keep you a few moments longer.

Be prepared for rejection. Be only concerned with your own inevitable rejection of self as death chooses not to claim you yet and life welcomes you, as always.

If it's written and destined and you are granted more moments, you'll be dashing off to Pops' house—eventually! To get long overdue crucial conversations to take place and DEMAND, if you dare, to finish each other's sentences. Have those conversations, clear the air, say sorry, and accept the apologies you may never get.

Be considerate though and imagine that you're the person who will find you. YOUR BEST UNDIES PLEASE! You may involuntarily shit yourself, so briefs would probably be the better option—they will hold more than that sexy G-string! Even if you shaved and wore your Victoria's Secret best, shit running down your legs is still shit running down your legs.

Sunglasses or something covering your eyes, please! Even if you think you closed them, eyeballs pop out of their sockets when sufficient pressure is applied. Never a pretty sight.

Get the height right! Quick snapping of the neck is preferred to avoid slow depletion of last breaths.

Method Two: Slashing of Wrists

It's all cute carving your arm to pieces, but for those needing finality as opposed to release, you must ensure that incisions made are VERTICAL and NOT HORIZONTALLY across the wrist. The incisions should preferably be deep enough to reach and sever the main vein blood highway. It seems bleeding out occurs quicker in a bathtub or basin of water. It takes mere minutes for the drainage cycle to complete.

Method Three: Gunshot

Early one Sunday morning, we were awoken by the sound of sirens and flashing red lights pulling into the driveway of the neighbors over the road. A mentally challenged daughter shot both her elderly parents then herself in the head. Only one parent survived, permanently handicapped, and the shooter ended up brain damaged in a wheelchair.

Head shots are messy. You have to know what you're doing to make sure you don't end up un-dead.

Many attempted gunshot suicides leave the victim alive, albeit ultimately comatose or retarded. The brain is a lot more resilient than you would imagine and the bone structures of the human body are a lot stronger. Even if the gun is on your temple or in your mouth before you pull the trigger, the recoil almost guarantees that it won't be in the right place when the bullet is ejected from the gun. You can easily remove part of your frontal lobe and still live.

Method Four: Gassing

Contrary to the widely held belief that one just falls

asleep, there have been instances where the capillaries in the face burst, eyeballs pop, and tongues swell so much that it protrudes from the mouth, leaving the jaw in a completely unnatural position.

Carbon monoxide works in the following way: hemoglobin, the body's way of carrying oxygen around the body, mistakes the monoxide ion for oxygen and absorbs it. The difference between oxygen and monoxide is that monoxide sticks to the hemoglobin, and isn't removed. This means that actual life-giving oxygen is no longer distributed throughout your body.

Remember that a car exhaust with a high CO level will be more deadly than car exhaust with a low CO level.

Those were just a few methods—there are many.

There are always reasons to suicide but there are also always reasons to not suicide.

In various religions, suicide is regarded in different ways. I often questioned the views and judgements so easily handed out, and often wondered whether these souls did, in fact, go to a different place. I always wanted to know where in the Holy Book it said that it was a sin or that it would receive the harshest judgement from God. I wondered if this was so and if I'd ever again see those loved ones that took flight.

When my husband took flight it was more comforting to adopt my belief that, in the final moments, it was between him and God anyway, and that we don't actually decide whether we live or die, and this is ultimately proven with the number of failed attempts.

I learned recently from another theologian that nowhere in the Bible does it speak of the things that we were made to think.

I am grateful to have my belief affirmed mostly by Neale Donald Walsch in his book, Home With God: In A Life That Never Ends, which reads:

'Two conditions must exist in order to classify a death as a suicide.

You must be aware of what you are doing That is, you must be making a conscious choice to die.

You must be making the choice to die for the purpose of escaping, rather than completing your life.'

He says further: 'Comfort may come from knowing the person who has committed suicide is all right. They are okay. They are loved and are never forsaken' and that 'they will simply not have achieved what they set out to do. That is important for anyone contemplating suicide to understand.

The sad thing is that those who end their own life imagine that they are going to change things, and they are not.

Ending your life in order to escape something does not create a situation in which you escape anything. If you are thinking of ending your life in order to avoid something. You should know that you are contemplating something that you cannot do.

A wish to avoid that which is painful, is normal. It is all part of the human dance. However, in this particular moment of that dance, a person is trying to push herself or himself away from something that the soul has come to the body to experience, not to escape.

Because that person has found the experiences to be painful and difficult, he or she seeks to step into a void, where there is nothing to face and nothing to fear. But people cannot step into a void, because there is no void to step into. A void does not exist.

What is the space filled with? Your own creation. You will face your creations wherever you go, and you cannot escape them - nor do you wish to because you have created your creations in order to recreate yourself. It will not benefit you, therefore, to attempt to sidestep them, or to dance around them. Dancing your way to the void cannot be done. A Void Dance is not possible,' and 'what you die with, you continue to live with.'

'You will encounter yourself on the other side of death, and all the stuff you carried with you will still be there.'

He goes on to share much but I am mostly encouraged that we get to see these angels again, too.

4: HUMAN TRAFFIC

"Why didn't you come find me?!" are the words that still echo in my head over and over. "Do you even know what I was going through!? You didn't even look!" Not the first words I expected to hear after the longest search and unimaginable sense of helplessness at not being able to do anything but wait as others searched. I know all too well the nightmares too many mothers go through when their child goes missing. Those and other nightmares still collide sometimes, albeit not as vividly.

I didn't know what to expect as we waited for the plane to arrive, but was so relieved to see her face as she stared blankly through me as I took her in my arms and just held her. It was the only thing I thought I could do to give her relief or comfort and let her know that the horror movie she had just survived and gotten herself out of was over. Or was it?

I happened to be online when the message "we've got her" appeared on my phone's screen. A friend I hadn't spoken to in six years appeared on my computer screen at the same time and asked if I'd found her yet, as she had only just seen the missing posters we'd posted too many days before. I told her I'd just received the text message and asked her if she could please go fetch "our daughter".

The tow truck driver who found her said he'd found her walking in the street, bleeding, a broken nose, and drugged out of her mind. He took her home to his wife, who cleaned her up, fed her, and gave her some clothes to wear. Another friend had left work in the meantime and took her to her sister's house until she could be fetched.

I spent an anxiously manic, but much relieved, afternoon at work until I could leave. Straight to the local pub where a group of friends waited with me for news.

When my friend called later while at the district surgeon, I asked her what had happened to my daughter. All she said was that there were some things a mother never needs to know, and that she was safe. She has still not told me about that crazy day.

I knew I had to get her home to me as soon as possible, quickly manifesting the necessary funds to send her 'other mother' to fly up to Johannesburg to fetch her and bring her home. There was no way she could fly unsupervised and a bus trip would take far too long only to deliver her back to the bus station where her hell began. I knew I had to mentally prepare for whatever lay ahead. A bottle of whiskey was the first temporary solace. I knew life would never be the same. I intuitively knew she would never be the same.

In the time she was missing, she was held by a sex trafficking syndicate, drugged and raped by more than forty men. She had needle marks all over her body, her nose broken, stab marks all along her spine, her nipples completely disfigured. She was molested and violated with knives, bottles, and whatever objects could be used in every orifice. I thank God she was drugged.

I silently watched the light in her eyes fade as her old zest for life quietened. Looking back at me were eyes of knowing, wisdom, enlightenment, but the warrior spirit had left little fight in the beautiful vessel that housed her once smiling soul. She had outgrown the world, and yearned only to flee from the vessel most would crave, but which had ultimately been the most dangerous thing to have and had caused more trouble for her than she knew it was worth.

While preparations were made to get her through the system and back home, I knew I could absolutely not rely on my own understanding alone and allowed myself to be guided to those Angels who would appear on request, or from nowhere, to lend assistance, guidance, comfort, and unconditional love, and ultimate healing. Those who were sent to hold our hands as we embarked on the journey down the many winding roads that lay ahead. The journey into, through, and out of the madness we had to undertake was difficult, confusing, heartbreakingly devastating, and took every bit of anything I may have had left, and I had to call on the wisdom of the ancients, whose words guide and comfort me still.

Life as we knew it stopped and its only focus became

the 24/7 "babysitting" schedule. I knew I could not do it alone and am grateful to the few who committed themselves to this and lovingly shared the moments that made loving her back to life possible.

After a series of visits to mental health professionals, counselors, healers, doctors, pastors and the like, my baby girl soon tired of most of these and started refusing any and all antipsychotic, depressant, or other mind-numbing medications that were immediately prescribed. These included antipsychotics, antidepressants, sleep medication, as well as antiretrovirals. She insisted upon weekly HIV tests. She opted only to smoke marijuana, which my GP agreed with rather than nothing at all, until she stopped that, too. Her dressing style changed as she opted for hoodies and jeans, little and then no jewelry or make-up, and the music she would previously play on repeat all through the long, sleepless nights to drown out the monsters under her bed and the unseen ones in her head, no longer played.

The silence that replaced the melodies was way more deafening than I'd ever heard or felt. Most days were spent in her darkened room until it was time for the folks to come home or her fiancé to visit.

The initial concern that she would roam around alone and get into trouble as others, perhaps seeing her vulnerability, could, would, and did take advantage of, was replaced with other concerns.

Baby-Girl had learnt to perfect the tough exterior

deception and was adamant she was getting better and back to normal as she attended to getting her things in order, including getting her dual citizenship for Spain. I'm one very proud Mom as she is sworn in and I'm putting together a resume and she starts job hunting. Gets a position at a local supermarket, insisting that she had to start contributing to the household, and wouldn't accept that it was good enough for me that she helped with chores if she was up to it. Not forever, but at least until she took however long it was needed for her to try to heal. Or was that break, I wonder in hindsight.

As weeks turned into months, under the facade of normalcy, it became apparent that things would, or couldn't possibly ever, be close to normal again. Her very core had been changed and the shapes and colors that once made a beautiful face smile had become an unseen and invisible blur on the horizon of the days that were once places of joy and all other good feelings.

At the same time, I was told that I was being transferred from where I loved to work to a different site. I was devastated. It felt like a whole planeload of my nearest and dearest had been wiped out in a plane crash. I decided to take all the leave I had available to recover from the shock and get the necessary meltdown survival preparation done. I would no longer be close to home or the doctor. Just in case.

Baby-Girl was not happy about the changes at all. The lease on our apartment was also coming to an end, and I hadn't managed to find the next place we'd call home. When she asked what we were going to do and where we were going, I assured her that she didn't have to worry about it and that it had to be a surprise and we had to follow where we had been led.

I was exhausted, depressed, and mad as hell as I tried in vain to make her feel anything other than freaked out about me moving.

The day I went back to work, she didn't wake when I popped my head in to say good morning, as she usually did. Neither did she follow me to work as she had been doing almost daily and didn't answer any of my messages the entire day. The last message she left was to her fiancé before midday. The grumbling in the pit of my stomach only got louder as the second hand on the clock I checked repeatedly seemed to freeze between the minutes, making the eight hours ahead seem like an eternity. I knew something was amiss as I could no longer intuitively feel her presence.

As I silently prayed that she was only having a sleepy day, I wondered if a broken-hearted prayer had been answered. I knew it was perhaps my turn to feel what God may have felt when he gave up his only son. I knew I had to do the same and entrust her soul to the next leg of her journey as the sight of her hanging, as her father had so many years before, greeted me when I unlocked the door and I knew that the time had arrived.

I once again found life cracking me open as I covered

her frozen self with a blue blanket and let myself slip into myself as I waited for hours until she was carried out in a yellow (or was that red) body bag.

Sia sings *Chandelier,* which becomes my daily fight song as I fall apart daily, hourly, and sometimes even every other minute on every unexpected occasion as I am forced to drive past graveyards at least twice a day to get to work. Even on the occasions when I thought I'd be working at a different site and would not have to endure seeing another mother lay flowers on a stone or clasping a marble tombstone at the head of her child's small, shallow grave.

I am challenged daily as I am horrified as young girls are misled, taken, captured, or enslaved to satisfy the whims of those men and women who support the industry of human trafficking. There are too many stories to not want to tell. I never got it or maybe I got it all and it's a sad, sad side of the world we live in. I can only pray it heals sooner rather than later.

Society has created a disease that sickens as it pleases. Fed only by the needs of those who insist on calling themselves human. Completely bastardizing the beautiful, mostly erotic, and amazing gift of sex and intimacy that we have blessed to be given to treasure and keep sacred. There is enough for all that is.

However, evil will persist and the easiest prey are those we neglect to pay attention to—our daughters and sons. Perhaps they get caught by being in the wrong place at the wrong time, perhaps they go looking for trouble on purpose, perhaps their drinks get spiked when they're not looking. Anything, whichever thing is absolutely possible and then happens. It is out there. It is real. It doesn't only happen to someone else's child. If you need to fuck someone younger than your own children, you need to look in the mirror. You disgust me. You need to be the person you want your own child to marry—not the monster that you are.

A million things could be said, but each must do their own homework into this insane industry that is still going to get way out of control before it gets better.

And for the parents that aren't paying attention to their children who are looking for an escape from a possible loveless, empty place that they can't call home: beware, there are places that will welcome them with open arms. Don't lose your child to these demons. Go get your kid and hug them and love them back to life.

The reality of these scenarios is that your daughter will never have to sit you down and tell you how the worst day was when the screaming babies stopped screaming. It was then that they were sacrificed. Or that on another day, she decided to let the other girl held captive with her have a break. "Take me instead, leave her alone," she would insist to her captors.

You will never have to watch her try to scratch herself out of the mirror of her nightmares, as a once beautiful body is now etched with eternal scars on skin you could not possibly want to have encasing your deadened self.

You would also not be left with only a social media page on which to leave her the notes that you'd find yourself writing from time to time:

My Dearest Baby-Girl,

Sweet Indigo Child, you were born trying to die even before you existed, and you knew I always knew that, with every smile you faked so well. I salute you for your bravery and your courage and for your insistence that you were everything I ever was and am still destined to be... Thank you for all the essences of you that were a mirror of me.

I still struggle sometimes to breathe and curse the tears that catch me unaware and can't swallow or talk because of the lump in my throat. I miss you dearly every day. When my feet hurt from miles of walking, I remember your long walk—the longest stretch of 145km's. I remember your broken feet and how proud you were of the journey you had taken and completed. You drove me crazy, you made me laugh, and you loved me most. I was honored that you chose me to love you back to life and to let you go and respected that you chose to take up residence in my heart instead, so that you too could set me free.

In so many dreams... you got off the bus... I found you sooner.... We watched many more full moons together and talked and laughed until I grew older as you kept me young. I no longer watch them alone as you sent me an angel to hold my hand and talk for hours and laugh like we used to. I'm making sense of it all and finding that thing inside that keeps me moving forward and making each day count for something. Even if it's just to make a lonely heart smile or eyes lighten up at the promise of a rainbow after the rain and always remembering to let the sun kiss my face.

People thought you crazy, even said you were on drugs as they unknowingly looked on and passed unfair judgment. I didn't care what people thought and ignored their glances and ignorant remarks. If only they knew, their comments may have been different. They may have understood and received you with the same love you so freely gave and shared with the world. A love that was just purely unconditional. The love you gave and never expected in return and trusted in the promises of the universe, even when the world repeatedly let you down, betrayed your trust and took your love for granted as it broke too many of its own promises.

Returning to the places where you left your whispers and sweetest breaths reminded me of all the messages you have entrusted me to pass on—be your voice and spread your light, the light that shines when I look in the mirror and your eyes look back at me and you remind me to keep going, through the darkest of days and longest of nights. You keep shining through. I am eternally grateful for twenty-one years of you.

All My Love,
Mommy

5: TWENTY-FOUR KICKS TO THE BACK & A FEW CAR ACCIDENTS

My whole life I have been doing a dance with my body even though I never was a dancer. Some said I always had a dancer's body, as if I'd been a ballerina all my life, flowing through life but so awkward throughout the journey with my body.

We're all on this amazing journey. We all journey our own exquisite way and only the author of that journey will be able to tell their story because only a few could comprehend another person's pain, or broken or imperfectly healthy, or was that another's perfectly unhealthy body.

It started from "pre-hatchling days". Besides a few beatings while pregnant with me, my mother was burnt with boiling hot oil from her stomach to her feet down the one side of her body. This would probably be the first major body shock to my unborn self.

I was run over by a car at five, at which stage I received my first taste of the stuff that numbs in a vial. About three months of medicated recovery time was needed while scars began taking up residence on the surface of my skin. Crossing the road was never the same and playing in the traffic took on a whole new meaning as my first phobia of traffic is etched into my psyche.

Enter the second reason for traffic phobia when I was nine years old, and a drunk driver came at us head-on around a mountain pass blind corner. We veered and, realizing he was about to go off the mountain, he swerved and t-boned into my side. I was flung into the driver's lap, having just taken the seatbelt off to stand up through the sunroof and let the wind blow in my hair. The car hit just as I sat down. Besides a small cut on the butt and a mild concussion, I was fine.

Two or three car accidents at later stages in life don't help to alleviate these for many years and a "BMW-sandwich" en route to work one morning at around twenty-one was a big instigator for years to come.

My life contained a myriad of clumsy, 'Calamity Jane' incidents of sometimes hysterical comedic proportions, even if only in hindsight.

Migraine headaches plagued me from very young. I remember being a frequent visitor to the nurses' station for a couple of aspirin from as little as about six years old.

My colon was often twisted, and intestinal maladies took their own turns, too. Measles, chicken pox, conjunctivitis, and frequent bouts of stuff being put on eyes for infections end up being faithful other remedies for many years to come.

Early visits to the dentist for the mercury fillings of the seventies ensured the first doses of Novacaine were administered around five years old.

Sugar could be put on anything and everything, and I am its biggest fan. Caffeine by the potful in marathon coffee-and-smoking afternoons were the order of most days for as long as I can recall and, I suppose, in keeping with those things that are handed down from generation to generation: story-time without the campfire, around Grandmother's dining room table.

The medical history is ridiculous! One would assume a form of hypochondria, but those bouts don't get you on the operating table for an almost yearly 'switch off', compliments of an anesthetist who gets to play God (or was that the grim Reaper's little helper?). My receptors start getting regular jolts and system reboots.

The list would contain in excess of a hundred areas of my body that needed some form of rewiring, removal, or replacement. I used to tease others about having "faulty wiring". I had no idea that I would be the one who ended up with more "faulty wiring" than most.

After a hysterectomy at 26 years old, I managed to wean myself off years of sleeping tablets and almost all painkillers, and upped my intake of vitamins and all supplements as a form of replacement medications. I was determined to steer as far away as possible from any medication. But this did not last for too long as time added a few more areas requiring a whole new range of pharmaceuticals to the menu.

The next surgical procedures in my thirties would be left and right-hand carpal tunnel surgeries two months apart. While the second wrist was still healing, the thumb was broken by the husband during a domestic disturbance.

Thirty years of migraine headaches cease to plague too many more days when the dentist removes four wisdom teeth and four molars, before I can be fitted with a bite plate to sleep with. This would in turn relieve muscle spasms down the side of my face and neck caused by grinding my teeth and clenching my jaw.

Then came internal shingles, regular IBS, a hiatus hernia, and occasional seasonal asthma. A frequent return visitor was the aftereffects of a whiplash injury sustained in a car accident in my early twenties, which regularly required physio and acupuncture.

There would be numerous 'body knocks' in between the health issues requiring medical attention, medication or a surgeon. More than twenty-four kicks to the back left me unable to sit for weeks after another domestic disturbance. Lasting, and possibly permanent, nerve damage to the coccyx area.

It is possible also during this incident that my hips were shifted out of alignment, but that could have also been due to a previous accident as a child. I didn't know the extent of the damage at the time as I quietly sat down on the donut ring cushion he brought me to use, and took more than the prescribed amount of painkillers to slip away into the deepest parts of my mind. It was very hard to keep my promise to my children, but I knew I would never leave them alone—and most definitely not with him.

Said previous possible contributing incident occurred when my sister and I were taking turns at riding someone's scooter up and down the road. All the kids were taking turns. Not knowing that when one is coming down a very steep hill towards a stop sign, you should start pushing the brakes a bit further back and definitely know how to pull the brakes without accelerating. Having had no previous experience, I swerved to avoid knocking my sister down as she tried to get me to stop because it was her turn. I drove straight into a neighbor's gate and was flung over it, left hanging like a rag doll folded in half. I recall feeling only as if I'd been punched in the stomach. Never reported this possible medical situation as we'd have to explain why we were riding the scooter underage and really wanted to avoid that lecture. This misalignment was only discovered by a body stress release practitioner in my forties.

I would find myself needing a third carpal tunnel surgery, months of physio, acupuncture, x-rays, and other tests, before the slow but steady onset of osteoarthritis and the need for a spinal fusion, which I politely declined. With no more medical insurance, the choice was to get better or wrestle with the public health system.

Mental Yoga and one stretch at a time and an absolute determination to get up and walk further than the corner of the garden was my starting point. I was missing out and had to spend far too much time alone to work on my OCD in a much smaller space while others got to go out and play.

Having weekly acupuncture and physio sessions are also

good therapies that help get our bodies the physical attention needed. But that's not always possible when we put ourselves out of civilization and the helicopter that was on order when things got shut down is still in the hangar.

I forced myself to walk more and further until I didn't need a walking stick anymore to help get myself up, and trip myself up. I used my legs to get me up. I am very grateful for always having strong, healthy legs to keep me going. I was determined at 45 to not use that walking stick for too many years. The stick itself nearly killed me too as I kept tripping over my newly acquired third leg—no wonder men are always tripping themselves (and us) up.

I had to constantly remind myself to keep my body as aligned as possible, until it is a completely natural and unforced thing to keep straight as is our bodies' natural intended design, anyway.

I tried to smoke less, which lasted for about half an hour! Haven't ever seriously thought about giving up until circulation issues started making long walks painful, sometimes impossible. For now, this still niggles and finds its way onto the other list of areas requiring healing, re-energizing and restoration.

The universe delivers a box of body parts made out of molds that could have been made from my own body in a box left behind by a craftsman from times gone by. I turn these into my own personal 'body vision board boards', as I remember another piece of my own advice I'd sometimes neglect to take or follow, instead focusing on healing my vessel so that I can perhaps spend the rest of my sojourn here healthier than the first half.

Another borrowed pair of glasses arrives after not having always had specs or contact lenses. I could actually see horses running along a beach, and I could see clearly. Sight restored! My glasses broke more than I could see for too many years. Note to my little girl self: listen to the adults when they say look away from the direct sun, it is hell on the eyes. Cataracts making their way across my eyes will need to be removed, eventually. Followed by checking out the heart murmur, the myelin sheaths around the nerves to the brain deteriorating, and the loss of circulation and/or feeling in my hands and my feet.

I successfully learnt to manage a myriad of intestinal issues I'd had since childhood until I was diagnosed with a hiatus hernia. My initial plea to the doctor was to please operate. I was tired of months and months of testing and trying medications which messed with other meds I may have needed for something else. He refused this surgery, indicating the risk of developing other complications.

There is absolutely nothing fun to be said about procedures such as a G-Scope or a barium enema. Thank you, G-Scope—you really were a challenge to the gag reflex!

After overcoming and restoring healing to whichever body parts have already been healed, I know that the few that may still present challenges and require a bit of extra effort and attention. I do, however, need to be more careful with myself until I am "fighting fit".

As my core strengthens and I keep at it, I am noticing an increase in pain-free moments, enabling me to get things of substance done as we exchange energy as reciprocation in an ideal world where money isn't the currency.

Seventeen surgical slices into my body (or was that eighteen? I no longer remember). More tablets than anybody should be able to ingest, process, and eliminate to free the system of all things chemical. I was no longer wanting painkillers or other meds the doctors were too often too quick to prescribe.

I knew a holistic healing was required where I had to get to a place where I know with increasing certainty that I am as whole as I can possibly be. So I can still be Mary Poppins in the very final episode of Mad Max, complete with leathers, a new Harley Davidson, and a magician's wand of my own.

I would find myself placing these on hold as I attended to the other breakdowns in my heart. That is, at least until a spider venom almost claimed two fingers, the left hand needing surgery and the right hand unusable for almost a year. Endless pain for more days than not while arthritis tries to claim the rest.

I swam in icy cold waters, melted under many African suns, walked until my feet couldn't take another step, and only when my health stopped me in my tracks did I allow myself to take the time to rest. Not that I had a choice. I could not move!

Besides the very occasional anti-inflammatory when pain was at a peak, the only medicine I used to treat the various conditions were natural remedies. Reiki, other healers, and plenty of prayers and meditations all played their role. We are sent the healers we need when we need them.

I had to keep my mind, my hands, and my heart filled with all things positive so I could get through any challenges which may arise.

The thought of getting the slightest cold or getting ill does not turn me on at all and I'm grateful to have kept the flu bugs at bay. I have to constantly be mindful of my health and the limits to which I can take my body, trying always to be as fit and physically strong as I am able.

I now rarely take medication, though some have hinted at a visit to the local psychologist, perhaps, as they are unable to accept that I am as okay as I can be, and that's great considering that which is behind me.

I am grateful daily for this vessel, even with all its quirks. It has taken many, many years to love it, after spending far too many under the impression that I was just another ugly duckling.

Whether I liked it or not, this would still not be the end, and my mind, heart, and soul were still strong enough to walk unaided. If you perchance pass by and I have a stick, it's possibly just the illusion of a little blue broomstick, no more and no less.

Don't be offended if I don't wave back or if it appears I'm giving you an odd look—I've probably sat on my glasses again and can see no further than the tips of my fingers. No disrespect intended.

Just come closer or wave and call my name.

6: LITTLE BLUE PILLS AND OTHER REMEDIES

What are little blue pills you may wonder? Performance enhancers, or were those pain suppressors? Things that numb.

They are those crutches we may find ourselves reaching for in the wee hours, when the rest of the world goes on a health kick, to the shrink, or all the other places that are nowhere near you, and they're legal. I became a Guinea Pig, trying anything that was strong, stronger, and the absolute strongest, after far too many years being handed a pill of one sort or another to deaden some or other pain.

Not only did my heart and my core need to be numbed but so did my actual pain body. Whichever part hurts at any particular time. Pain killers. "Killers" being the operative word. I was determined to avoid going under the knife again so, instead, I kept the pages of my doctor's prescription pads well inked.

I loved energy tonics in my twenties when the Coke, cheeseburger and chocolate slab would become an almost daily breakfast. I love food. One would think I would have turned out to be the little Lotta in the family, but was more like Twiggy, or whichever nickname I collected or earned, asking the way through a rather clumsy co-existence with my body and it's two left feet.

Too many visits to the doctor would result in me having spent more than enough years in altered, yet completely functional, states of being. This would go from existing in a haze of the highest schedule medicated haze I could find through to no medication at all.

The list went on and I, like many others, knew all too well the most effective combinations of those easily obtainable scripts.

In later years, a friend would tell me that the bottles of tonics I lived on were the same as doing speed. I stopped because I would never do the speed I'd only ever heard about or saw on television. Some years on, I would go down that road too, until too many friends had too many strokes, and I watched different addictions claim different lives.

Initially, I couldn't understand all the hype about illegal narcotics and was never really too easily taken with or by the need for more than I had gotten legally viz-a-vis the prescription pad at the end of my doctor's pen.

It was inevitable that I would start experimenting with those other recreational stimulants in my thirties.

More health issues meant more medication. Prescribed, over-the-counter, and self-medication. The illegals gave me energy and the ability to overlook and overcome what the legals no longer could. By this stage, my tolerance levels were so high, I always needed more than the usual and double shots were the order of most days.

For the longest time, whiskey, beer, wine, or anything alcoholic were merely replacements for energy tonics, coke, coffee, and all the other things I had eliminated.

In the dead of night, the loudest noise could be the turning of the page (or was that the bending of a page?) in an attempt to see the words formed on an unlined page by the light of a silvery moon, long since greyed over by the anticipated rain clouds that tease and taunt with a few occasional drops of water to wet your whistle.

"Pour me another drink, barman!" was a familiar request.

I don't think I've spent more time looking into the same fridge for more hours than I care to admit, as I often contemplated how many more years I would attempt to sip away at bottomless glasses of beer, which were always topped up during the once-in-a-while pee breaks. The glass doors always contained reflections—or were those reflections the holograms of the many of those who chose to share the many streams of that golden liquid sunshine with us?

Sleep will not come on another morning after the most recent night spent contemplating the years of too many unspoken things, perhaps shared with the best friend many of us shared: the bartender. The one who was occasionally allowed the time to share a favorite glass of their preferred liquid honey-colored streams, boldly displayed, urging and enticing and encouraging us to imbibe and share our spirit. At this junction, the aforementioned bar-person would make up for all the time spent ensuring our spirits were level—or was that levelled out?

In fifteen years, I hardly missed a trip to go to watch some or other sporting event, which I never really watched. Preferring rather the distraction of a hologram or twenty others in the reflections of the glass bar fridge door.

I overindulged. I had to try more than enough letters in the alphabet soup of narcotics, till they too bored me and served only to keep me awake and alert enough to bury myself in a very busy world of work and at home, while my body started (or stopped) doing its thing and my husband his own. I could hazard a guess of about twenty years of recreational substance consumption. It made the other silent, unspoken stuff a little bit bearable.

This, I now know, only kept me safely held in the arms of denial or rejection of said stuff as much as possible. Somewhere along the way, I learnt to say "it didn't hurt me", as I programmed myself to believe that 'I am never broken' as Jewel kindly reminded me in her song Hands.

The Universe© let me know that I didn't "come here to face hurdle after hurdle after hurdle. It's not as if by mastering my issues today, more issues would be added tomorrow. That would only happen when I denied them today. I needed to master my issues today and be free. I needed to get through what I had to get through today and understand what troubles me, today. I needed to do what I could today and the rest would be made easy."

As I clumsily let go of the attachments to those little blue pills, I needed to detach from in order to completely and holistically restore myself. I had to learn different and new more effective ways to be. Be what? I wasn't always completely sure because there were so many things that could fall under that umbrella. I knew it had to be the best version of myself.

Birds start singing before the breaking of the dawn because they instinctively know there is always light after the darkness of every long night. Faith in what just is. I knew that I had to be like birds and keep my faith, no matter what.

"Every addiction arises from an unconscious refusal to face and move through your own pain. Every addiction starts with pain and ends with pain. Whatever the substance you are addicted to—alcohol, food, legal or illegal drugs, or a person—you are using something or somebody to cover up your pain. That is why, after the initial euphoria has passed, there is so much unhappiness, so much pain in intimate relationships. They do not cause pain and unhappiness. They bring out the pain and unhappiness that is already in you. Every addiction does that. Every addiction reaches a point where it does not work for you anymore, and then you feel the pain more intensely than ever." ~*Eckhart Tolle, The Power of Now*~

Out went alcohol, drugs (both prescribed and illegal) and most over indulgences.

In came breath, faith, trust, respect, praise, acceptance, kindness, compassion and love in all its completeness and absoluteness.

I still have a backup little blue pill for the sometimes-still-too-hard days which take my breath away and need a bit of help from the pharmacist, but only a mild, manageable extra. But only until I am allowed out of my room while the world keeps its humans indoors and within the borders dividing ourselves from one another.

I knew there would always be "times in life when things simply needed replacing because they get tired, broken, worn out, harmful, outdated or irrelevant. I found myself being pushed to take stock of the things that no longer served my best and highest good, so I could replace them with things which did and do." ~*Susan Young*~

The Universe© reassured me on another day that "no matter how scared, tired or ill I was; no matter how lost, confused or desperate I became; no matter how lonely, depressed or cranky I felt, if I just did what I could with what I had, from right where I was, it would always be enough."

I wish I had learnt this long before all that liquid food, which my unraveled soul no longer seeks, and which was replaced and replenished by the air I am blessed to still be able to breathe.

I now know the odd drink I may choose to have from

time to time is no longer more than just that; and reminds me that life will always be full of celebrations and I want to remember all of them! With champagne!

Cheers!

7:   ARRIVING FROM THE DARKNESS

There's a Native American tale about a grandfather who is talking to his grandchildren about life: "Inside each of us, there's a fight going on between two wolves. One wolf represents fear, anger, envy, sorrow, regret, self-pity, resentment, guilt, inferiority, lies and ego. The other stands for joy, peace, love, confidence, humility, kindness, friendship, truth, compassion and faith." One of the children, pondering what his grandfather had just said, asked, "Which wolf will win?" The grandfather simply replies, "The one that you feed."

I kept this little tale on a small scrap of paper for many years and referred to it often—and still do. I had to remind myself to do my best to feed the right wolf. I did not always succeed and, in fact, first had to let the other one get fattened up, almost obese, before it needed a strict regime of diet, exercise, and a massive character readjustment. I could do that only after life had given more than its fair share of trying to beat it into me, or was that out of me?

I vowed that, no matter my own personal demons or perhaps morbid fascination with my own dark places, I could not go back there and would never do that to my children again or leave them as orphans, even when I later found myself in spaces when I least wanted to live.

I had a choice: I could choose to wallow in self-pity, regret, guilt and all that other stuff, or I could move forward in faith—even when, at times, I may perhaps have questioned what, if anything, I believed in anymore. There had to be something that continued to guide me towards whichever destination I was being led. Or was it that I was the one who was, in fact, being taught and guided to lead those with the same questions as I had, or just to accept that there may be no answers to those questions?

The search for answers or guidance to help my girls get through such a tragic heartache from so young, led me down many avenues as I studied volumes upon volumes of pages of mental health information, watched tons of whatever I could find to teach me or guide me. Counsellors? We tried a few. It was, however, difficult to find the right counsellors, who I was adamant would at least have to have some life (and loss) experience before they would be in any position to add value to the healing process my children would find themselves having to go through. I found myself in the unfortunate position of having to teach my girls young that people go away and hearts get broken. That it was part of the natural rhythm of life.

This, while I simultaneously had to learn how to manage life with husband number two, who turned out to be a stepfather from hell, an abuser who hid behind alcoholic memory lapses. I accepted his denial that he needed to be treated for a bi-polar condition (or whichever label one could attach). It became an unmanageable chaos too many times of the week, which would eventually end in ruin as the girls got older, tougher, and independent enough to leave home and make sure that I too eventually left after he almost succeeded in killing me as his enraged Mr. Hyde-self consumed his Dr. Jekyll?

Take some time off, my mother insisted.

At forty, a way was made for my escape and I found myself packing my life into a 23kg bag and headed 'home'. I'd been offered a 'paid' holiday on a one-way ticket for as long as I wanted. Mom was making sure this time that I would be tempted to stay longer than my usual short stay-overs home. We could catch up and make up for many years apart. I had lived a life not many knew about back home and I had, by this stage, many years of practice at having my "I'm fine" smile ready.

Little did I know at the time that we would only have eighteen months before our borrowed moments would be over as life got cut short and hearts are hardened as they are repeatedly broken and exposed to life after death, and life again.

As I started emerging from the darker spaces in my life, I found myself pausing for one last reflection of the things on the other side of the threshold of promise. The journey that had spanned my life of fifty-something years contained a myriad of events, learning, blessings, loss, challenges, and has covered many landscapes. Having freed myself of all things physical and material, I was able to deal with just me, the face in the mirror that I never really looked at or really saw.

I don't know why I was always afraid to face myself until the blessing of real, honest, raw, divine, agape love showed me how. Love nudged and shouted at me to pay attention and accept all those things that he sees I am. I am still at times intimidated by the pedestal that he's placed me on and is adamant I am worthy of the position. Some days, it takes me longer to really feel it and to step back into that self that I have become, or am constantly becoming.

No one would expect, least of all me, that something so pure would merge from such a dark place, or that from the keeper of the hands of time would emerge the compass that would lead me through the writing of this book and to the eventual unbecoming of another me from times gone past.

As I looked at the face in a picture I had produced, I noted that I had unconsciously blanked out the eyes which no longer just stared out blankly, but seemed to have had its sight restored and could really see me. I felt a sense of needing someone's acceptance or validation and looked around. Only for a fleeting moment, though, as I realized that it truly had nothing to do with what anyone but me had to think or say. The only acceptance and validation I ever needed or required was my very own.

The darkness I attracted, or was possibly born into, had always seemed a safer place, even if only because it somehow seemed familiar. I needed to be put in those spaces in order to really know what those spaces were all about, though at the time the reasons would not be so clear. Or was it to attract those lost souls that I was to guide, protect, and hold their hand as I walked them home, whichever home they chose to go to?

I often found myself somehow doing your typical, or not-so-typical, re-enactment of Julia Roberts' character in *Eat Pray Love*, as I made my way across many landscapes, some not the most ideal, in search of something, some place or state of being that would finally feel like home. I knew I could not do it alone.

It started with a prayer, or perhaps another silent scream, as the rain fell softly on my uncovered self at the foot of a tired, old tree that seemed to lean into me. Or perhaps I was leaning into it.

"I Resign!" were the only words I could form on the page and signed my name as silent, hot tears burned my cheek on their way down my face and collided with raindrops and the world became a murky blur, for every minute of the few hours that had passed by unnoticed.

I decided that the only way I was going to get things out of my head was to address a formal query to the 'Big Guy'. Who else was I to ask in this deserted forest where I was the sole inhabitant? Passersby didn't see me. No one knew that I had fallen off and was no longer there. It read:

Dear God,

Please help! Just a little old me, feeling really, really hurt. And I really don't sympathize too well.

I have so many questions, but now I won't ever find all the answers. One definite one though would be, WHY ME??!

I know I have this really good, pure heart. Why then only borrow my love and keep ripping it away? My name does apparently mean fit 'to be loved', not hurt.

What were those lessons all about, anyway? I remember having been tested on most of them before. Did I get the answers wrong? I really did study hard and the practical near killed me and left me needing a bit more than a little alternative healing therapies, natural products, and an extra big, extra sticky, extra thick Band-Aid sponsorship.

Anyway, enough about that, I can hear the ice cream truck driving down the road... How often do we chase promises of soft serve, but by the time we get it, it has been melted down by the elements.

Maybe I am only watching this movie and collecting stories. All I would love to do is go home... where I belong—and I don't even know if that's in existence.....
Where is that elusive thing called 'home', anyway?

Okay, so that was more than one question..... The others have all been answered, those that were meant to be anyway.

Please take me home. Loneliness sucks!

I await my report card at your leisure—as I have mastered patience, as is seemingly a pass requirement for this leg of the course of this evolution that has been my allotted subject.

Thanks,
Me

No-one was coming to fetch me and I was only getting soaked sitting under that old tree in the rain, with no sunshine or rainbow in sight. Apparently, it was time to, once again, toughen up and hit the road. With a weakened body, I no longer felt as agile and confident to use it as its own weapon when I needed it the most. I also knew that the last little blue pill I'd saved for the minute I bungee jumped into my all inevitable 'next', had long since worn off, as I quietly crept out the nearest door as if I was just popping down to the market for supplies.

Who knew where I thought I was going. I just knew that, when you think you've had enough and you've reached the end of the line you never dared cross, you now have no choice.

The next note said: Next Destination: Everywhere!

A million thoughts raced through my head. Where did I think I'd get with not a cent to my name, no phone, or even a jacket? It didn't matter, as I no longer really cared. I was tired of everything. Who would notice I was wandering around a village that had long ago been my home, but no longer was.

It was getting dark and with no-one to call. I found myself returning from the 'market', climbing into a hot bath, and in a complete void climbed into bed and pulled the covers over my head, ignoring any questions or the absence of them. Me just having a grieving mother moment. "She'll come around soon enough," I knew would be the response as I dragged myself through, up, and out of another dark day.

I could be angry but instead choose to be slow to anger and, in times gone by, I found it all too easy to say nothing or simply walk away, and walk away far enough to leave my perceptions or illusions of how I thought I'd been 'wronged'. Perhaps I should have let my truth out more often than not to avoid too much time spent as that proverbial doormat and allowing too many to take my kindness for weakness. Perhaps if I started voicing my opinion more harshly than perhaps necessary. However, these outbursts were never really about standing up for the real things that may have offended me. If I had, I guess I would let some know that I may have been 'angry' because (fill in the blanks yourself).

I didn't want any of it and didn't know if I had it in me to get through the ups and downs of yet another relationship. A relationship which was 'new enough' to give up on, run away from, and leave behind. I had too much 'stuff' for anyone to be able to be comfortable enough to hold my hand through, or for anyone to even believe that I had dealt with most of it. I had heard too many times that I was in denial and only acted 'tough'. I felt I needed to release him from me. Another heartbreak seemed to make more 'logical' sense. But I couldn't leave him, while he had no idea that I was fading and running out of the 'stuff' that had gotten me this far. I didn't know if I could be the one to lift him out of his own nightmare, or to help him heal the wounds and fill the gaping hole left by the loss of his own beautiful mother. I couldn't fix everything! I was tired! I wanted to give up.

I was sure that my absence would be no different to how absent I already was and felt in the spaces that I found myself occupying. I then remembered a long ago silent promise that I had made and even though my daughters were all grown up and carrying on with their own lives, I could still not leave them behind with no parents. I could also not let the succession of down days keep me there, anymore.

"What now, God?" I asked as I looked around for a sign, any sign of what to do next.

"Get up, get dressed, get out," I heard the now all too familiar daily voice in my head that I tried to block out initially, especially on the harder days when all I wanted to do was disappear into myself and not have to stick a foot out of bed, let alone face a world I no longer felt part of.

The Universe© cautioned me to let the need for a sign be the "sign" that I should make haste very s-l-o-w-l-y and consider this a "sign" that perhaps, for the moment, no decision should be made."

Almost mechanically, I started to rise and move one foot in front of the other, trudging my way up, through and out of the muddied world I had found myself in. I knew that this is what I had to do for however long it would take to return a sense of normalcy to my core. I had to start re-energizing my life, redirecting my focus, and restarting the engine. Some minor adjustments, slight dent removal and panel beating was possibly required.

Along the lines of my life, I found myself drowning in crowded loneliness which threatened to consume and engulf me. The threat of my hands (or any other part of my body) possibly no longer working loomed closer as each day passed. I had to consider the only possible alternative: To step up, step forward and say something! Anything!

Sometimes, when it's too quiet, we may find ourselves seeking out some noise, if for no other reason than it's louder than the noise in our own heads. We choose the next steps. The ones that we may have avoided for too long, but realize the time is now, so we may as well start stepping up, stepping forward, and owning what is rightfully ours.

"Speak Up," I heard myself say. "But please, speak softly, for should you speak too loud or shout, I may not hear you above the noise in my head or that of your voice."

There's always a moment of chaos before the calm. I knew that I needed to let everything go and see what was left behind. At the end of the day, there was too much stuff in the way and I couldn't see myself anymore, let alone the wood for the trees.

The broken, and as yet unspoken, bits were left amongst the chaos. The unspoken bits in between those things that hardened as they softened and would ultimately lend themselves to unlearning and healing.

And so we start collecting masks to wear and seek refuge behind as we learn to only very rarely unmask our true authentic selves, pushing us closer to the edge as the inevitable next arrives unexpectedly, as it always did and usually will.

We had no fixed routine, mostly because we were artists and had become used to odd hours and enjoyed the comforts (or un-comforts) and freedom to create as we were inspired, as long as we turned what we loved doing into a smile, we were being our authentic selves.

I went on a whole load of road trips, soon learning that backpackers, boarding houses, and even living with the kids, isn't ideal. They all have very different ideas about bedtimes which do not suit the artist/creative who may like to go for ice cream at 10pm (pre-curfew) or a midnight stroll on the beach. I loved that about that little town that became too small, or perhaps too big for itself. I knew we had to go where we were divinely guided to go, without question.

At the foot of a different mountain, just alongside another beaten track, a rusty and tired old train track glistened in the sunlight akin to a long, slithering mirage. I find myself in the almost-out-of-there-section once again as I learn a hard lesson that, sometimes, my part in any particular hero's life story isn't to catch or mend a broken heart, but to clear a space; an earthly, divine space.

"If you have to, just pretend. Make believe. Fake it. Right now, get up, walk outside, smile, wave, wink, and exude," The Universe© offered up its seemingly not very well thought-out defense mechanism.

I should get a medal from the acting school for getting the 'fake it till you make it' strategy down to an award-winning performance. The proverbial red carpet was definitely being prepared for my arrival.

I still have the wind knocked out of my sails unexpectedly sometimes as life throws a surprise punch, but my six-pack is way more defined, so I can pack whatever punches are perhaps heading my way. Not only that, but I learned many things about the power, or powerlessness, of a punch.

I read somewhere that when expanding out of our comfort zones, we should choose excitement over fear. These similar feelings could lead one of us to struggle and the other to curiosity. I needed to embrace staying with myself on the adventure, and would find myself holding my own hand as I frequently found myself being directed to travel into the unknown. Trying to always be safe and secure in the face of the mysteries was not always possible. I was, eventually, guided to find the willingness to harness the strength of tenderness and the wisdom of discomfort, as I uncovered my own misguided promises made, kept and broken.

A blank canvas on which to create a new life was handed to me—I just had to find the right paintbrush with which to create the right textures and shades I wanted to fill my life with.

I may start at the first, last, or any stroke in-between.

8: FIRSTS, LASTS AND INEVITABLE NEXTS

First, I instinctively knew that I had to lose it all before spaces to find 'it' were made, and I could fill the void left behind by the act of shedding it all. It seemed an impossibly massive void, and I sought to do my best not to fill any part of it with any of the stuff that had clearly not worked. The only 'stuff' that could come along were the trusted, tried, proven and guaranteed things. A note appears before my eyes that reminds me, 'old ways won't open new doors'.

I grabbed another Friday's list of stuff to do and headed out. I found myself in a shopping mall on a Friday afternoon in Johannesburg eight-and-a-half years after leaving city life behind and heading for the hills. Many faceless strangers made up the ocean before my eyes as I strained to see if there was anyone I recognized in the city I had decided to return to. But, the only familiarities were geographical, as everyone seemed to have moved out of town.

In eight years, I had lost count of the many miles I had travelled in my absence. Not for a minute had the thought crossed my mind, or even begun to consider, that others too could, and had, long since moved on.

The start of another new year, the first one without the loved one who would never again share or be there for the celebrations, is always the hardest and most challenging. I found myself contemplating the start of another year starting off so gut wrenchingly sad, alone with no idea to think, feel or aspire to, as the craving to be held for a few fleeting moments seemed too overwhelming to even breathe, or the energy to draw in a breath. I sat for longer than the shadows could hide or dissolve my tears, with the ebb and flow of each wave that crashed upon the not-so-deserted shore I found myself clawing toward in some vain attempt to escape.

I found myself just focusing on getting through and out of the inevitable 'nexts' until I no longer make apologies for remembering an angelversary, a birthday, a fond memory, or even those that weren't so fond. Eventually, I would get to a place where I no longer needed 'grief share' but wanted and could encourage more life share.

We miss 'things', but not things in the material sense of the word. We miss a laugh, a special hug or a kiss on the forehead from a never-forgotten soul who went ahead, not being able to say goodbye because we didn't know it would be necessary or that it would be denied. Perhaps because it's never really goodbye and they never really leave, they only change shape and join the ranks of all those other unseen "things" that hold worlds and hearts together.

Life felt different, constantly changing as it always had and always would, and I was different. I felt new. I felt ancient. I felt timeless and ready to step out of the 'almost' section and start making check marks alongside those things on whichever bucket list I chose to look at.

Striving to achieve 'Mukti' (freedom from financial consciousness) enabled me to reach a deeper, more meaningful place, where all the world's abundance seemed an archaic settlement amount as it's all mine anyway, and no amount of money or possessions could fix everything and neither could it replace things lost to the hands of time.

I wrote those letters to my loved ones who went before, some I never could, and perhaps never will. I listened to the sad songs, loved the love songs, and danced to the rest even if I didn't particularly like the songs. I allowed myself to not feel bad about no longer clearly remembering what someone's face looked like without looking at a photograph as time clouds my mind. I am constantly learning to dance in as many moments as possible.

I inevitably slipped into the role of counsellor and friend to many as I learned to be braver and allowed my re-lit self to shed light in some of life's darkened spaces.

I heard somewhere that 'when you can tell your story without crying, you've healed'. For the most part, I have and am proud to be here sharing these things with you. For the other parts, my bravest self will allow me to embrace the human in me and I'll shed more unexpected tears, without shame.

There's no grieving period.

When you're ready, you'll lift your head and you'll allow

the sun to defrost your frozen self. You'll find what you have to read, do what you need to do to help you continue through the rest of your days without your loved ones. You'll reach out and be reached for. You will be held. We hold each other. As we should, as we must.

Just allow yourself to be yourself. Be gentle.

And when the day-to-day realities of life apply the usual pressures, deal with them one at a time. Know always, you've got this.

I'm always mindful that it could always be the last time, so I make a point of that embrace, that kiss, that whisper, that smile, that wink, or that wave, every time.

If that's not the way it ended and there were things unspoken left in the way, know that these too get healed, perhaps even answered.

Inevitable next? Time has taught me to choose, to never ask what's next, and to just embrace this moment as the next one which I may have wondered about yesterday because it's always today and the time is always now.

9: LIAR, LIAR

Lies are bitter pills. Don't keep things from anyone, especially your children or parents, because time will either age it like a fine red wine, or it can become vinegar, too bitter to swallow if left to mature for too long. We leave it on the shelf and it's usually left to become another dusty old bottle on a forgotten shelf. That is, until an unexpected visitor to the wine cellar takes it down, dusts it off, and pops the cork to reveal nothing but the rancid odor of long since fermented contents.

This may be a most bitter pill to swallow for the deceiver, having to admit the lie and for the deceived a most painful, yet forgivable betrayal, once understood, as lies have wings and can fly far and wide, until their eventual return home to the place of origin: the first foul breath.

The Universe© suggests I "try to understand the truth and that little can yield so much: a new perspective, an admission, a surrender to truth - however painful - changes everything as another mentor cautions that not knowing leads to knowing. Knowing it all leads to not knowing anything."

One can tell a warm hug from a fake hug straight away. There's such a lack of genuine hugs. Rather don't hug me. I won't be insulted by your un-affection just because you don't know how to give it. You see a person really trying to deliver warmth, but they're so cold within themselves. You could get the warmest hug from the coldest soul. The person that is holding you in their mask of warmth can be warm, yet so very cold. Sometimes it's hard to tell when something appears real at face value, especially when we ourselves have learned to master hiding.

If I look at your face, how am I going to know if you're warm or cold, as you have learnt to show your warmth, but your eyes are an ice-cold blue?

Is my core warm or cold? Do I have an icy core? What is required to melt my core? Can you stare at me long enough to melt my core, or will I melt yours? And if I had to let it go, what would remain behind? A melted core?

We expect life to be easy or self-explanatory, plain sailing or transparent, and perhaps for the few in the minority it is. But sometimes there is an inconsistency in the flatness of everything. We thought we would have sensed it, but we have to first hone our senses and train ourselves to use our intuition and gut feelings, which are usually never wrong.

We have to first go through a process of learning to re-trust—starting with ourselves, if nobody else. It is only in the moment of re-trusting that we notice what we should have perhaps picked up on before. As it goes with most things, it never happens in our own time. So when, out of the nowheres and long forgotten remnants of the faded secrets or lies we pushed into the farthest recesses of ourselves for whatever reason, we are returned to the mirrors of deception we refused or neglected to look in, and are left with no option but to stare these in the face and do the necessary. Failing which, we are returned to these same places recurrently until we find what leads us to grace.

One could use the analogy of pulling thorns out by the roots and not just the parts sticking out of the earth's surface. We need to learn sooner or later to keep the soil as pristine as possible to ensure the best grapes grow, unhindered, in order to produce the bottles of wine to be stored, cared for, and loved to maturity, and to the eventual placement on that old wine shelf in some collector's cellar. We really have to ensure that we really bully those old roots deep down, giving more than just a slight yank to get them out. I'm no expert at horticulture, but I do know something about weeding and pulling out the roots of fields of thorns. Those buggers are down deep and sometimes need real excavation and super strength to get out. We avoid thorns which seemingly have no purpose save to encapsulate and strangle, stab, and smother. We may too often think we need to excavate to expose and remove. We do whatever we can to attain the desired 'perfect' state. Alas, this excavation reveals new and not always such exciting information that we buried beneath the surface of all the veils and illusions that time wrapped its loving hands around and claimed.

There will naturally be those things that need, want, or

should remain hidden and kept where they are perhaps safer and silent. There are those things too that are also sacred and which must be entrusted to those who would be the ones who would prove to be worthy guardians.

I was blessed with the gift of wisdom from an early age and a great intuition, which was usually right, but I was too shy and perhaps petrified to risk really being confirmed as the family nutter. So, I learned to wait for natural courses to play out enough times until I knew instinctively whether there was a lie, falsehood, or hidden agenda present.

I would also have to go through those times that most face: having to deal with lies. Life would call upon us to encounter and confront this thing, either by not saying a word, or saying something in a roundabout way, or through omission. This seemed to exonerate and or dispel the need for one of the worst labels or characteristics we may have needed to willingly, unwillingly, consciously or unconsciously experience, mostly to please others and to keep our fragile human ego's from ever possibly being put in the same category as the ones who blatantly and unashamedly throw those lies about as if they were nothing resembling the placebos we would have preferred.

I always hated lies, especially ones that I would later in life come to realize were not me being so honest and trustful, after all. I would be more focused on keeping my promises at whatever cost, even when I had promised to protect another's lie or untold/unspoken secret. I hated it even more when I had to knowingly omit or lie to protect the ones we love because we also wanted to try our best to keep faces and reputations intact. After all, what would 'they' think?

We risked perhaps hurting another's heart or revealing a different other's long kept secret involvement. They too may be found out for their own discretions which may be the polar opposite of what they are, when they're keeping themselves hidden.

We have to pay attention to, and become more aware and conscious of, all our senses and not only hear, but really listen to ourselves.

One of Neale Donald Walsch's lines, "There is something here I do not know, the knowing of which could change everything" makes me seek out more information, be patient a little longer, and let things reveal themselves as they always do and most surely must. This will serve to avoid the risk of another awful, misinformed assumption that perhaps, just maybe, it should be understood that I can completely admit when I am wrong and even apologize if I cause any harm or offense. This doesn't happen too often and, if it seemingly does, it's because I didn't want you to see I noticed it all and pretended I missed it. I absorbed it all; especially the ones no-one else saw or wanted to look at.

I had learned that the only way to stay in intimate relationships is to go towards the discomfort and share what is in the secret chambers of our hearts. I knew that if I wanted to experience true belonging, I had to show that which I would usually hide.

To enable release and relief, I knew I had to speak the words I had for too long held silent and face those things that had over years got stuck in my throat. My Reiki healer let me know that my throat chakra was completely blocked as she took on my healing as her own. I needed to learn how to speak up. Not just about life in general, but specifically about the things that really got buried when, somewhere along the line, I decided to rather keep silent and keep the peace instead of disrupting anyone's peace, because I had so long ago tired of the noise. It was easier to just not say anything and let 'the others' think they were right and/or just agreed to disagree. Knowing, perhaps, that fading into the grey spaces between the rigid black and white lines (or squiggles) others swore were the only ones to follow, that there was no in between.

I found myself considering all the times I had faded to grey and had shrunk myself to accommodate the disrespect or disdain of others, and knew only much later in life that this would only serve to cause me to disrespect myself and regard the reflections in the mirrors I so consciously avoided with the utmost disdain. We are, after all, sometimes our own worst judges and jurors, and I am no different.

The words still stop on choke as I consider what it would look like if we did actually speak our deepest truths.

Would I reveal one or other family's shame, lie, crime, judgement, misdemeanor, unkind or brutal act, by saying the things that weren't necessarily mine to carry or cover up, but had been given to me regardless, and the world insisted (I naively thought for too long) was my obligation to have and hold?

You would never guess the middle child was, in fact, the firstborn who would only learn it too late—and still remain silent to never dishonor her mother or another. She would never have the opportunity to be looked at like only a first born could or would be looked at by a father. She will wait until the afterlife where promises kept would ensure she would get that look in the next life. The promise to keep another's secret to protect another's lie or shame should have been reconsidered and/or forgotten. Perhaps it should never have been revealed to avoid more pain to the innocent bystanders. Or perhaps it needed to reveal the true characters of those who played puppet master behind the scenes.

You would never know that, just maybe, that friendly young man you assumed was just another homeless beggar would rather be misjudged and labelled as a crazy druggie (or worse); was only there doing that because a jealous, controlling, and perhaps resentful father had enjoyed a lavish lifestyle of abundance and ease; using up all that guy's inheritance his mother left him. He would never shame his father and only ever wanted his approval and/or five minutes more of his attention so he could maybe remember what having Dad around felt like, so he said nothing. He humbly stood in line with others at the soup kitchen and was grateful for the food parcels distributed by the local church. Shaming him with the completely inaccurate accusation that he was responsible for his mother's death kept him in his shameful place of self-destruction, need, and denial. A homeless millionaire wandered about finding comfort, solace, and near destruction amongst those other wandering souls who are there because of some untruth someone else, or they themselves, had unknowingly gotten bound up in.

He would not be the only one. There are other stories of homeless millionaires who ended up there because of the lies of others, or of their own. I learned to just not be too quick to judge.

Another 'misfit' was unable to find the stuff in him which would ever get over a broken heart when his wife left him for another, as life and lies on the streets lead him to start believing that "he who makes a beast of himself takes away the pain of being a man". I still reach out to him, even if he refuses my hand. He is sick and perhaps his craving for it to come to an end may overpower that last glimmer of hope in his eyes that prays for a different reality.

"Remember that when things don't go according to plan, they go according to truth. No matter how painful the reality, it is reality nonetheless. There is dignity in facing the truth without trying to cut it down to a more manageable size.

"There is honor in acceptance." ~ *Vironika Tugaleva*~

Most people tell them: big ones, little ones, white ones,

black ones and maybe even some blue lies. Not all our truths are pretty, believable, and definitely not worthy of a re-run or repeat, but until we understand that they'll remain ugly, or unbelievable, and insistently repeat them until they are seen, digested, and believed.

Or not.

10:   FROM THEN TILL NOW
AND NOW TILL THEN

Or should it be from now until when, but what about then? It won't matter in the end and is all resolved and/or answered when it reveals itself to answer those questions. Well, some of them anyway. However, there are a few missing bits which, if not included, would result in more questions and leave a few too many holes for the imagination to wonder about or make incorrect assumptions as to any particular occurrence.

Where did the road take me? To places where I learned from the great and sat with the broken, listened intently to mother nature, and cast my eyes upon many sunsets and sunrises along many shores.

What was I trying to find? It could have been a million things or nothing in particular. Perhaps all I was doing was merely just being and allowing myself to be found by whoever or whatever needed to find me.

I had to learn to fill the time freed up by my own empty nest in the absence of the busyness of a home filled with the sound of children after twenty-three years spent in 'domestic bliss'. I had to learn how to be content by myself, not be afraid of me, and learn to enjoy my own company.

In the moments when solitude perhaps could and did overwhelm and silence deafen, the ringing of the midday church bell served up its daily reminder that time was still passing whether I was paying attention or not.

I attached more meaning to the words 'time to wake up' as lunch time became wake-up time. Having usually only fallen to sleep during the wee hours of the morning, this became the norm rather than the exception.

The void left by the choice not to spend all my free hours at the local watering hole, left me with endless hours freed up, with fewer rooms to tidy, fewer plates to wash or let pile up on the kitchen counter, and no wet towels to pick up off the bathroom floor.

Post-meltdown, I decided to take a sabbatical from work and without a concrete plan, except maybe to get some sunshine and do lots of walking, talking, keeping silent, screaming, weeping, writing, praying, and breathing. In these moments, I learnt freedom from time in the conventional nine-to-five sense, as I accepted that the time is always now. I can only ever be in the present. I threw out the alarm clock, switched off the news, and went offline.

This was no act. It is my life, and there will still be more rehearsals.

I had learned that when circumstances or disappointments bumped me off track; it was the beginning of even bigger dreams coming true, which could not have come true on the track I was on.

I learned from a young age that "what lies behind us

and what lies before us are tiny matters compared to what lies within us," as perfectly penned by Ralph Waldo Emerson way back in the 18th century.

I'd come far with my physical and health challenges, and I became more aware that I no longer had reason to delay. I was no longer required to avoid sorting out those things that no longer needed to tug at the heart.

I attended those chat sessions and am still doing the work that needs to be done as and when it appears in my reality. I have all the time in the world, or not. I know that I need to heal what I take with my soul. Heal that, and the rest may just fall in or out of place.

All the emotional bits in between the moments of chaos, or between each kick to the back, have all been fused back together again and are held together by the unbreakable faith of this woman that I am constantly aware and grateful I have become and am able to be at your service.

I read somewhere that "healing is about coming into harmony and peace in your heart. Healing is a kind of grace, where you learn to embrace the state of your body and the struggles of your mind while turning your attention to where the totality of your being meets the wind and the stars and the sunshine. You are much more than your physical body or your thoughts".

In a fraction of time, the world is turned upside down, inside out and back to front. Nothing stays the same, even when we're holding on with all our might. Instinct tells us to fight, as wisdom tells us to just breathe and let the things of the world fade from sight.

The world is sent home to start tracking the numbers and watching the statistics change the numbers on a daily basis as we are banned from life as we know it.

Locked down.

As we inhale a breath, and hold onto the one thing that will see us through all things and that is The One that guides, loves and protects us, never giving us more than we handle.

I've lost count of how many days/weeks/months/ moments we have been forced to sit back and witness in absolute amazement, shock and horror as the world shut itself down, as Mother Earth pulls rank and repossesses herself. She gets to decide how much breath she needs to purify, to recover from thousands of years of going through everything one could possibly imagine at the hands of too many millions of us who thought the 'others' were the perpetrators and they the victims of something someone else did or didn't do or say.

As she inhales it all, she blesses, restores, forgives, extracts, deletes, wipes clean, and renews every last blemish, poison, insult, or whatever thing each one of us contributed towards her inevitable destruction and near extinction, being the only choice left if her very core was to be preserved.

Full moon cycles ebbed and flowed as sure as the oceans' tides and she exhaled the purest, newest first breath over and around and into all those who would walk upon and be the caretakers and gatekeepers of the "Grandmother" of this planet we call home.

In *The Surrogate*, Tania Carver writes, "He had once read somewhere that a writer had suggested six seasons instead of four, with the extra two either side of winter. Locking and unlocking, he proposed they be called. A time when the world closed itself up, clutched itself in something more like death than hibernation."

We had to go through a testing and qualification process to ensure that all inhabitants were of sound mind, healthy intelligence, strength, resilience, endurance, and respected all the guidelines laid down to prevent the need to CTRL+ALT+DEL our systems to restore factory settings, defrag and re-sync the systems to ensure clarity, preservation and the sustaining of the amended requirements. And that was merely to be let in the front gate and led up a path that looked the same as we always knew, but it was so much clearer, straighter and free of bumps, potholes or debris. A luminescent glow, strangely warm, seemed to echo and magnify the newness of an old road.

Membership forms, contracts, responsibilities, and service delivery requirements would all need to be completed, signed, and agreed to prior to inhabitants being handed their keys to this new earth.

For failing or neglecting to listen to her whispers, which eventually became deafening screams followed by a desperate wailing, we were all grounded and sent to our rooms like little children. No amount of tantrums or stamping of feet got us anywhere and served only to have our restrictions harshened until we, too, felt like our breath had been taken away and that we really had to make friends with the walls around us.

A myriad of emotions and reactions, ranging from shock, fear, complete panic and total denial that this was not only affecting us in our own little bubble, but the whole world was systematically shut down, one country at a time.

From now until then, I guess I am sticking with my decision to let my life be divinely guided by the best movie director ever: God/Me. We are one and there will always be footprints in the sand as we carry each other and hold our heads high as we remember to bow them, too.

"There are no accidents, no coincidences, and no strangers", The Universe© lets me know for certain as "the perfection of your every 'issue' is beyond human comprehension". Don't be fooled. You've made no mistakes. The territory behind you and the challenges at hand were precisely crafted to deliver the wisdom and insights that'll make possible the most joyful time of your life, so far.

I knew that I'd know when I needed to know, and not a moment earlier. The Universe© had let me know that "this is how it works when the answer you're looking for depends on other events that must first settle, new players that need to be gathered, and serendipities that are still being calculated."

"The presumption, at all times and under all circumstances, should always be that you are good enough, worthy enough, and lovable enough. And that you are exactly the right kind of person, in the right place, at the right time. Otherwise, you wouldn't have been instilled with such dreams in the first place."

I often wondered where 'home' was, and sometimes still do as I get ready to pack and move onto the next location. Destination unplanned as I am led to the next place where I'm just in time to catch a falling heart—or was that a few?

"What we do and who we touch has rippling effect on society." ~*IndiPam*~

11:   GOD'S POSTAL SERVICE

I met a man in a church one day. He was a guest speaker, a clairvoyant, and a spiritualist. He swam with dolphins. An Angel in denim jeans, leather jacket, and boots and helmet. I no longer remember exactly what message he had delivered to the parishioners, but I was moved enough to wait behind after most of the other churchgoers had left the building, to thank him.

I recall a younger me being mystified and most curious at the message he delivered just for me and wondered if I'd ever swim with dolphins; as I navigated my way around the judicial system for a protection order.

"You have a white aura all around you. It's connected directly to God and every essence of your spirit," I recall him saying. He then told me he saw me being a teacher, but not in a classroom. He saw me "sitting in the hills with many children around me." I loved the sound of that, though I'd never imagined such a picture as, by that time, in my not-so-early thirties, I had only experienced most of which would probably be the very opposite thing to the seemingly idealistic picture that was conjured up and placed deep in the core of me. It served to teasingly confuse me often as I was tempted to 'jump ship' or, at the very least, voluntarily institutionalize myself into the long beckoning delusion of rest beyond those other walls where we sometimes have no option but to drag ourselves over to, sometimes voluntarily.

I often found myself praying that I wouldn't really end up as crazy looking as I some days perhaps felt. That picture was sent to the forgotten archives at the top of a long, winding, and very sinister-looking staircase, which seemed to lead itself to a red door, behind which were protected and preserved secret forgotten closets of ghosts. Another me searched everywhere and nowhere all at once for the elusive hills which evaded my line of sight as I ensnared myself in the valleys between and below.

The picture soon faded and lay dormant and forgotten in the decades that would be served up by the 'Time Master'.

Only when I found myself being returned to a forgotten place by coincidence, at a time I most needed to be reminded of the long forgotten picture, now most certainly safely cocooned in a blanket of dust on a top shelf of the archive.

"A dusty old picture on a shelf… The glass is all misty, my own true self..." I vaguely recall the words of a poem I once wrote a good few lifetimes ago.

As I made a mental note to eventually return to the archive to retrieve the contents, I thought perhaps (and silently hoped) that the paper had been consumed by the sands of time.

A psychic channels a letter from the other side from Mom. It reads:

"You are my bravest daughter. No challenge is too big for you—you are a true warrior woman. There have been many, many, many souls that have entered and exited your life in ways that are almost unimaginable. You have honored each with so much reverence. Each one of them never knew that anyone really could see them. You did. Each and every one of them. You saw them in a way that they were unable to see themselves. Your ability to see so deeply into a person's soul heart can only be matched by your sheer bravery that is willing to look. Not many people are able to see into someone with such depth that you come with. The joy you bring to the table is off this planet. When you enter into a space, you are able to beckon that laughter out from deep within a person. Many people are surprised that they still had it in them to laugh so hard. You remind those who have forgotten of their young spirit. This makes them feel comforted in the face of their aging bodies. When you leave, your presence lingers on within the space you occupied, filling it with lightness and joy. Many people need you to be reminded how joyful life can be. And it is the simplest of things that can bring joy into your world. Look at the rainbows, look at the butterflies, they are all around you. You remind people to look up to the sky, when all they have been doing is looking down to the ground.

This, my girl, is your greatest gift.

I love you to the bitter end
XXX"

"Cut! Cut! Cut!" a voice echoes in the recesses of an old, abandoned building.

"Hello," said God. "Are you ready for your interview?" is all I remember as I jumped out of bed, realizing that it was just a dream.

This led me to contemplate and imagine that it really was the day for my "interview". I needed to ensure that I would always be ready when He/She called my name and, even if I did drink one too many glasses of Merlot than the recommended daily allowance, there would be no time for hangovers. I had decided to call God by the name of "Scotty" for the day, hoping frantically that he'd beam me up.

The Universe© delivers a note: "Today I'll be recording your every thought and emotion, no matter how 'good' or 'bad', no matter how generous or stingy, and no matter how helpful or hurtful they may be. And everything I record will be played back for you as soon as possible."

I went through the mini mental list of questions I tried to anticipate could possibly be asked during an interview for the position of a lifetime as I imagined the quiet shimmering flashes of 'heat lightning' in the night sky as

'Scotty' took pictures. I remembered reading that 'Scotty' "takes pictures of everything you're doing, so you'd better behave yourself because one day there will be the final judgement and these pictures will be passed around for all to see" (Patricia Cornwell, *Blow*). I could only imagine what the photo album would look like.

As usual, I let the clues fall into my lap, getting my cues from the song 'What if God was one of us?'

My first response would be, "oh but she is," as I imagined God as a Redhead with a pink Lady Gaga Stetson on her head and heeled cowgirl boots, guitar in hand, as the band began to play indicating the start of the interview.

I would get to decide the questions, too.

Oh, how different the journey would have been if I did indeed join the nunnery. The exam/interview would be much less complicated as the list of sins of the Sisters would only require one Hail Mary and one Our Father prayer to suffice as penance to absolve. The closest encounters with the ladies of the cloth have only been Whoopi Goldberg in *Sister Act* as she sang 'My Guy'.

The church our grandmother took us to, only had priests, elders and altar boys. Perhaps this is what inevitably led me to not being entirely convinced to keep Catholicism as my only "religion" of choice.

Needing only to be reminded later down the line and for the rest of this eternal life that my religion is Kindness. I had mastered focus and was no longer living on empty. I had been made acutely aware that revelation seldom comes along the expected lines and I was, and always had been, accepting my call toward the eternal progression of my soul in order that I may light the way for others to be reminded, too.

I knew that a hundred 'Hail Mary's' after each Saturday evening's confession wouldn't clear me for the following morning's sharing of blessed bread, after anointing with Holy Water or oil (depending on which date it was in whichever holy calendar or whichever place of worship) and that would grant me absolution and I could partake in the 'blood of Christ'. In most places of worship, this 'blood' was disappointingly only watered down grape juice and not the rich fullness of the red wine they first tried to convince me was my 'Big Brother's' blood. Alas, I recall as too many years have filled the space, that perhaps those were maybe the leftover sips of my dad's wine during the Saturday morning clean-ups after the adult Friday night get-togethers? I no longer remember. A case of selective Alzheimer's is starting to sound strangely amusing and appealing. No disrespect ever intended to those going through this most difficult experience. There are just some things one may choose to send to the 'Forgetter' in all of us much sooner than the 'Rememberer' in us is prepared to.

After communion we heard many sales pitches that putting two hundred bucks in the bag as your 'tithe' every Sunday didn't do much more than pay for the coffee or feed a select few members of the community, and an untaxed salary for the pastor in the latest threads. Lockdown would ensure that I too became that member of the community who needed and received help from the congregation who had been able to maintain their 'tithe' while economic crises knocked on the doors of the world.

In some countries, people drink from a golden chalice instead of doing things differently. Drinking from the same well as the villagers who stood outside and waited in line for their half ration just outside the gates of the holy man's very own city. Let the golden chalices be exchanged for the 'enough' that there is for each one of us who forms part of the ONE that we are, would impress me more. One can only hope.

I asked God for a raincheck because even though I was ready to answer any question; I wasn't quite prepared to be assigned the task of deciding on the questions.

These questions would be different. I would be asking myself to pass my own test.

I guess one of the questions would be: "What did you do with the gift I gave you?"

And, in the pause, we write more letters to God and await his reply, during which time his Angels keep us comforted with random messages. We learn to speak the matters of the heart unashamedly as we keep our end of the bargain and ensure we send the odd letter or note over to God's postal service for dispatch. We always get replies, we just have to listen. Be still and listen.

Dear God,

Too many times, maybe not enough, you tapped me on the shoulder to remind me you were there. However, too many times (and definitely enough) the devil tapped me on the other shoulder to tempt me with his wares. For all the times I failed you, I apologize knowing it's been "paid in full".

For all the times I didn't, I am most grateful. For the many chances you gave and fetched me out of the proverbial graves I may have been digging myself into, I thank you most sincerely or I may not have lived to tell the tales.

I thank you for the suicidal lives I have been able to save and for the strength to bear those that I grieved and carried home to you. I thank you for the many angels who carried me through the darkest times when my own wings were broken and I was unable to rise, let alone fly.

The promises made and kept, those that needed to be broken in order for the truth to be set free, proved the most challenging and behind which I hid for longer than I can recall.

You taught me to be the healer and the healed and blessed me with the knowledge and wisdom of many masters gone before as visions passed on to me by the ancients that appeared in the ink across many scrolls, remain as vivid as ever and I am humbled to be entrusted with both protecting some and passing on the rest.

You taught me young and at every age that I should be still and know that I needed to just let go and let you do what you do. The tests you put before me were sometimes grueling, exhausting, murderous and mind blowing, especially when I was an unwilling recipient—there were subjects that completely sucked and drew little or no interest for me as I often wondered how, never mind why, I got through those 'classes'.

Five decades, fifty years, or 650 lunar cycles, I have watched, studied, tested and delved into, through and around many facets of human nature and nature itself and found myself testing you too as my faith was tested. Time after time you met me right where I stood and I knew eventually that I need never have doubted or tested you and that your intentions for my life were so much greater than I could ever imagine, as I learned to shed my skin, shake off the old and embrace each and every new.

Though I know there are still potholes, bumps and bends in the road leading the way home, I am certain that my navigation skills are enough to tackle these too, knowing that I am the 'captain of my soul and the master of my own fate' and that your love and divinity is with me and had never left.

I offer my deepest gratitude for an answered prayer that brought my child both home to you as you continue to fill the voids left by her physical absence with life, love and peace, with each breath I breathe. I do miss the sounds of her laughter, though.

For so many years, I felt our fathers had collectively 'wronged' us until I realized, for sure, that you are the only father we ever needed and that not all earthly fathers got the message and that's okay, too.

You've shown me so much, I have literally been blinded by the light and know as I always have, that I need only remember to be still and know that my life is divinely guided and I need only look up, within and around my own self and I'll always find you there.

Thank you in advance for the strength to get through the harder days when crazy memories sometimes still roam around in my head, especially on those days that my smile is still sometimes unbearably hard to wear.

And the rest is all up to you.

Love,

M

The Universe© let me know that it had to "throw in a few valleys so that I could truly appreciate the peaks. A few scaly, ugly, biting creatures, to make the others more adorable. Some slippery slopes, dangerous curves, and moving targets, to show me how agile, brilliant, and cunning I am. Add a few more seasons in which slumber is as scarce as rain in a desert to help me appreciate a stolen nap, an evening stroll, and quiet times." I consider myself blessed that the universe had "dreamed up some pretty special people with perspectives and traits so unlike my own that sometimes it would seem my means of surviving the relationship would be learning to love myself even more".

For each and every time I thought I'd neared the end of my rope and could no longer hold on, there was always another rope being thrown in for me to hold onto. Those ropes were usually the ones that had been wrapped around the words that were either kept from me until I was ready to receive the wisdom of their meaning or until I was ready to uncover my own divine truths.

I am humbled and really grateful for rain checks, as I sure do have more than a few questions to ask myself.

12:   I AM WHY: REFLECTIONS OF A SOUL ON PURPOSE

My path would cross with a gentleman who I was told by someone was known as the 'Famous Addict'. Apparently, he was 'famous' or at least well known. He wrote a book. I'd never heard of him and hadn't heard of his book. Many subjects were covered during our conversation that lasted about five hours. It was the first time in absolute ages that I found myself listening intently, with as few interruptions as possible. I knew that this was an important part of the course and a perfect example of "when the student is ready, the teacher appears", as I learnt early from Robin Sharma.

I couldn't get enough of what he had to share with me and found myself sharing little or nothing with him.

He reminded me of a story I'd heard before about a woman who was trapped in her house during a flood. She'd refused to leave, even after neighbors, firemen and others repeatedly urged her to get out of the house before she was washed away with it. As the water started licking her feet, she cried, "God, why don't you save me?"

God replied, "Oh, but I tried, my child. I sent your neighbor, a few firemen and even a boat, and you refused my help every time."

This got me thinking about all the angels I'd been sent over the course of my life as I tried to navigate my own way through various and too many crazy, dangerous and potentially perilous incidents until I found myself on my knees again.

"Go out and be that angel", I heard a voice whisper as a gale force wind exited the scene of another unusual early morning.

"I had to break you to show you why I created you. You had to endure and go through it all so that you could fulfil your purpose as you learn and teach that we should 'bear one another's burdens," the voice continued.

Every person we meet is another rung up the ladders of our lives. They all form part of the interlinking that lend themselves to each other to enable the Little Jack in all of us to reach the top of that beanstalk as we rise again and again to meet our Giant. Some may call him God, others Source or Higher Power, but, for this chapter, I'll call him Mike and he/she knows that there is absolutely no disrespect intended, because after all, doesn't everybody want to be "Like Mike".

The Universe© again assured me and insisted that I was "sent to make a difference, to be a bridge, to light the way, by living the truths that have been revealed to me, so that others might do the same."

She insists: "Life doesn't happen to you... You happen to life."

It wasn't easy at first, but I came to know that one of the greatest gifts I could give my loved ones and myself is the freedom to learn our lessons at our own pace. The same applies to those who get on my nerves.

In revealing myself to myself, I dare never again hide any part of myself that would otherwise enshroud the un-shaming of my former selves, as these too are apparently necessary aspects to expose and expel.

Each choice I would face needed to be made with the mind of the highest within myself. Whether it be an act of faith, a crossroads or a decision.

I needed to find opportunity in every setback, disappointment and heartbreak and therein I would find its gift because everything has a reason and, if I looked close enough, that reason would always be love.

"You cannot get through a single day without having an impact on the world around you. What you do makes a difference, and you have to decide what kind of difference you want to make." ~*Jane Goodall*~

Many times I wondered "Why me?" Until someone asked "Why not you?" I had carved enough into and out of myself to be able to get the information I needed to get through the lifetimes I've been gifted with.

There is not enough paper to put down in words the state of perfect and peaceful bliss I find myself in. All those empty spaces that occupied too much of my time are now perfectly filled with imperfect moments. Nothing can touch it or bruise it, the petals now strong enough after having weathered all the storms. The colors bloom bright and luminescent for all time, whether dark or light, dim or bright.

There's not much else that could be laid before me that I would be unable to tolerate, bear, or withstand. I always stand humble before my challenges in the knowledge that I am able, I am enlightened, and I am me. Having overcome all previous challenges, my spirit remains unbroken, my soul free, and the presence of love that laid all bare and restored my faith in the belief that with LOVE all things are possible.

Life is beautiful and everything is what it's cracked up to be, but only once we smash the reflections and we are able to see through the cracks and face our former shatterings.

I learned that what I was being led to, directly connected with the agenda of my soul. That agenda is ever changing and in my anticipated promotion to 'Chair of the Boards', it will be no different and that's fine, too.

As I learn to honor and humble myself, I know that part of this agenda is to be a guide. I knew I had to speak properly, only cussing when absolutely fucking necessary. (If it's in the dictionary, I can surely use the word.)

We can all access eternal wisdom. We are all being inspired by the Source all the time. It is possible for divinely guided and/or inspired people to make errors, and make them often. Not every word or every utterance of the Pope or action by Mother Teresa was their right and perfect action; and Hitler could have gone to 'Heaven', too.

> Moments of Grace
> Found me in every place
> And all my fears disappeared
> Without a trace
>
> The wildest waters calmed
> Left me cleansed
> And mostly unharmed
> Ready to live a life filled
> With all things charmed
>
> I stepped outside
> The skies had cleared
> Making way for the rainbow's end
> At last, I knew, I no longer have to hide. ~ *Storme* ~

I knew and had met some angels who had chosen cleverly disguised lives just to help people get past judging by appearances. They weren't much to look at, listen to, or dance with, and most would never guess they're angels, but I guess that's the point.

It is part of nature's built-in checks and balances, that while there may have been times when I thought I couldn't even help myself, it was precisely in these moments that there was someone else nearby who I could help instead. After all, my angels had never disappointed when I least expected or thought I deserved. I always knew that this was the fastest way to feel better and that the easiest way to make the biggest difference in the world was to start with reaching out, right away, to those nearest. They happen to always be ready.

> Even if you counted all the grains of sand on earth,
> you still would not be able to understand God
> ~*Srila Prabhupada, Science of Self Realization*~

Nobody is who they are based upon any one decision, any one day, or one anything else, and that every day is a new day and life never stops or starts or re-starts, as it does.

Like the Eagle, my spirit cannot be tamed. Many tried, whether intentionally or not, to break my spirit. It probably did eventually show signs of wear-and-tear, which sometimes gave some the misperception that I could be taken advantage of in a weakened state. So 'they' did, as I inevitably allowed, albeit perhaps sometimes under duress.

My soul is my number one faithful friend, companion, guide, teacher, student, my undoing. My healing.

> "We cannot lose once we realize that everything has been designed to teach us Holiness"
> ~*Donald Nichol*~

I am guided to share these things with you because I guess I wanted to be a testimony to those who are perhaps weary from their journey, discouraged or disheartened that we get through 'this'.

Always remember that

"Love is Patient, Love is Kind. It does not envy, it does not boast, it is not proud. It is not rude, it is not self-seeking, it is not easily angered, it keeps no record of wrongs. Love does not delight in evil, but rejoices with the truth. It always protects, always trusts, always hopes, always perseveres."

As the Church bells ring, Jenny the steam train proudly sounds her horn as she goes through the town blocking the crossing. Those anxiously late parishioners being called to practice patience as they anticipated the possible reprimand from the Pastor, who would more than likely smile and greet you with a wink, just to remind you that God always waits.

Just get there.

13: ANOTHER NOTE TO SELF

I never expected to not make it to the Post Office to collect the note that would give me a heads-up for the next season of incidents and accidents which was filled with much laughter till the cheeks hurt and the tummies tightened allowed our smiles to return and turn the lifelines along our brows to smile lines. I got there, and it was closed. I would have to wing it.

"Lost in transit," the Postmaster would say.

It would have served well to read:

Hello Soul,

I'm not sure where one even begins to put words to the next journeys you'll take into the valleys of time and space and so very many things that fill you with grace.

You couldn't possibly have chosen a life of *"Further Along The Road Less Travelled"* if you tried as you once again consider changing your name to something completely different, like Gypsy Dawn, and in doing so forever seal the seeds and secrets I have given you to be uncovered, unkempt, understood, undermined, and held sacred.

You will need a few books as your list of teachers and students grows. The knowledge and wisdom that you will gain will be ancient and new as you are guided to be among the builders of the foundation for the next age, a forerunner of the light. You will be one who veils, yet reveals. You will be a dispenser of time as you lighten others' loads and lives and give them time, space, clarity and purpose in a world that threatens daily to completely consume itself.

You would be kindest to yourself if you remembered the things in between the photographs we remembered or forgot to take from time to time, too easily or too late. The grey spaces matter, too. Where fifty shades may hold and keep us in bondage for longer than it took for us to eventually remember the 'safe word'. When we eventually did, it would prove to be wonderful and magnificent and nothing we had not imagined, and so very much more.

Somewhere along the way, you left behind some stuff in a box in a shed. One day ahead of yourself and you'll remember how much you actually liked yourself. You'll go back to get that box and finally, when you're ready, you'll open it and reveal, embrace and celebrate the you that you kept hiding from. Throw out the bits that no longer served, be free to do, and be whatever you dream.

But first, you would have had to shed your selfless skin and know for sure that the time had once again arrived at that place where you could re-affirm that most of those things had been fixed. Those parts of you that were imperfect had been healed and now manifested as imperfectly perfect.

Even if you were broken down into mere suggestions of the fragments of your put-together cracked self, you'd be just as beautiful as any un-cracked porcelain mask you could think of covering your face.

The right teachers, mentors, guides and healers fortunately did arrive in time to teach so very many things that would guard and guide you to and through all the extreme experiences that loving yourself back to life would require.

In the middle of a random day, a butterfly tattooed on the arm of another young Earth child makes her way into the tapestry of colors of the pictures that now appear on a once lonely, blank canvas.

You are inspired as strangers call out to each other and figure out the dynamics of being dynamic enough to co-exist with the friends who ultimately become the family we choose. As time fades, so does it fade the familial ties that perhaps once bound us to obligatory loyalty and we find that we are safely and genuinely held in the spaces that aren't occupied by relations but by those friends that become the family we choose. These are our soul tribes where loyalty, love, and mutual respect are choices and not obligations too often demanded by kin.

The black sheep have to gather somewhere.

Life served you a tossed salad of reasons you could have had to justify a suicide of your own, but you somehow found a way to add enough dressing to enable you to digest the chunkier and least savory bits without slicing your throat to shreds.

It can all be loved back to life if we let it, and it happens each time you smile when it hurts the most.

I'm still holding the energy of the space.

I'm still wondering if you found yourself while I searched and found my own way back to mine.

I'm still wondering if you believe in the power of love like I know.

If not, my wish is that it loves you back to life.

I'm still wondering.

I'm still wandering.

Don't try anything once. Try everything one last time.

And another seven years pass in a blink and I look down at a book in my hands where Benjamin Franklin reminds me:

"Those things that hurt, instruct."

Rest in peace, Old Self. I'll never forget you.

With Respect.

14: PARTING WAYS

There's something about just knowing, I think to myself, as a gentle breeze caresses my cheek, silencing the sound of a Harley Davidson, hungry and growling its way through the middle of my morning.

Everything's according to plan and I continue to figure it out as the world turns around as she does, each and every time she takes our breath away.

We rise from the ashes, and thunder clouds bring rain to wash it all away, lightning bolts included. Clouds part, making way for rainbows, butterflies, and flowers.

It will never all be said or done. I just know that I know what must be known.

I close my eyes and imagine on another day the feeling of having both man and his machine between my legs as we silence ourselves in unified awe of another perfectly beautiful sunset, a sky full of stars, and the enigma of the rest of the road ahead. The one that goes everywhere.

I feel a road trip coming on!

The end (for now)

ABOUT THE AUTHOR

Amanda has spent most of her life in South Africa. In her lifetime she has experienced the loss of more than a few loved ones in various ways and too many to suicide. As a young mother, it was her husband, and as a grandmother, she would lose her youngest daughter, with many others in between.

On the other side of the masks she wore to get through the days that were meant to break her, she found her way through many of life's challenges including health issues, depression, divorce, abuse, addictions and unimaginable grief. And she still finds a reason to get up, try and share a smile with the world

Suicide Salad – Amanda White

www.ingramcontent.com/pod-product-compliance
Lightning Source LLC
Chambersburg PA
CBHW061147040426
42445CB00013B/1594